This Book

has been presented to the

CHURCH LIBRARY

MEET THE REAL JESUS

Bill Chitwood

BROADMAN PRESS
Nashville, Tennessee

4281-29

ISBN: 0-8054-8129-X

Dewey Decimal Classification: 232

Subject heading: JESUS CHRIST

Library of Congress Catalog Card Number: 76-14631

Printed in the United States of America

To
My Mother
Who
Lives in His Presence

PREFACE

Hello. I'm glad you picked up this book. And I'm glad you opened it to this page. I have a question to ask you: Do you know Jesus?

Wait! Don't answer right off. I do not mean do you know some dim reflection of him that has come to you through the haze of hearsay and tradition. But do you know him as he really was and is—as he thought and lived and loved and died?

God has given me the blessed privilege of inquiring into his mind—his attitudes and the convictions by which he lived and died. In this holy inquiry I have met the real Jesus who lived in and through the man. I have felt the heartbeat of the One whose sandals left their imprint on the sands of Galilee for all time.

My pilgrimage has carried me into the holy place of the Most High. I have often heard the voice of God speaking through the soul of his Son. Again and again, I have put off my shoes for I have found myself alone in the sanctuary with the Savior.

And now I bid you to come along with me through these pages. Perhaps together we shall have the joyous experience of discovering again the real Jesus. We shall go quietly along the way. And we shall stop often to meditate on this exciting man and to gaze on his radiance. It may please God to help us so that as we behold his glory, we shall be changed into his same image.

I owe a great debt to all who have shared this journey with me and to Jo Fooshee who faithfully for Christ's sake typed this manuscript.

CONTENTS

1

MESSENGER OF GOD

Long shadows crept in at the door of a carpenter shop in Nazareth. It was getting late, and the carpenter was tired. Hunger pinched his stomach as the aroma of the evening meal drifted through the window. He wiped his sweat-streaked face and brushed the sawdust off his clothes. His day's work was done.

The carpenter looked longingly around the little shop that had been his home for so many years. He carefully put every tool in its place, then took off his apron and put it away. He fastened the tool cabinets, walked out the door, took one last look around, and closed the shop never to open it again.

Tomorrow Jesus would leave Nazareth for the Jordan and his meeting with destiny. A strange tugging at his heart told him that the hour had come to begin the work he was born to do.

Who was this carpenter from Nazareth who crossed the pages of history over nineteen hundred years ago? Jesus, himself, put the question clearly, "Whom say ye that I am?" (Matt. 16:15). Each of us must answer this question for he is there—an indelible mark on the pages of human history.

Tacitus, the Roman historian, said:

"Christus, from whom the name—'Christian'—had its origin,

suffered extreme penalty during the reign of Tiberius at the hand of one of our Procurators, Pontius Pilate; and a most mischievous superstition, thus checked for a moment, again broke out, not only in Judea, the first source of the evil, but even in Rome, where all things hideous, and shameful, from every part of the world, find their center and become popular."

The Jewish historian, Flavius Josephus, states:

"At this time there was a wise man who was called Jesus. And his conduct was good, and he was known to be virtuous. And many people from among the Jews and other nations became his disciples. Pilate condemned him to be crucified and to die.

"And those who had become his disciples did not abandon his discipleship. They reported that he had appeared to them three days after his crucifixion and that he was alive: accordingly he was perhaps the Messiah concerning whom the prophets have recounted wonders."

You cannot ignore Jesus; you cannot erase him. You must decide whom *you* shall say that he is: Jew? Galilean? Prophet mighty in word and deed? Unparalleled teacher? Will you confess him to be true deity, the only begotten Son of God, the Messiah? Or will you join his enemies that snap at his heels like hungry wolves crying, "fake, liar, deceiver, madman, deluded soul, blasphemer"?

You must choose one or the other. He is either the Son from heaven or the blasphemer from Nazareth. Certain it is, he cannot be both. Either the Jews or Jesus was right. And we each take our place according to our convictions. We either march to his crucifixion or we parade to his exaltation.

"*Aut Deus aut non bonus* (either God or not good)" still stands.

Jesus was either all that he claimed to be or he was the world's most notorious deceiver and blasphemer. Jesus either stands as the exalted Son of God or sinks into infamy beyond our wildest imagination. And if he be not the Son of God, then away with him. I agree with George Bernard Shaw who said, "Better to declare the throne of God empty than to set a liar and a fool on it."

But could any thinking man suppose that so preposterous a deceiver, such a malignant person (as some suppose Jesus to be) could have swayed the world for nineteen hundred years? Could he have raised derelicts from the gutter or caused magnificent churches, hospitals, and colleges to be built in his honor and for his service? Could he have, by the preaching of his name, caused prisons to be reformed, orphanages to be built, humane rules of war to be drafted, and sane men and women for centuries to give their possessions and lives in sacrifice for his cause?

Whatever estimate you put upon Jesus, the least you can say is that he was a unique, dynamic, exalted person who shocked organized religion, staggered his contemporaries, and set in motion forces that have literally changed the world. His life, character, deeds, and teachings are not the ramblings of a madman or the carefully contrived cunning of a liar.

His teachings, deeds, and life are so extraordinary that his deity is a truth impossible for him or any other to deny. The Jesus of the Gospels is totally incompatible with anyone other than God.

He hushed raging storms, healed the multitudes, and fed the hungry. He raised the dead and lifted ruined lives back to usefulness. And when the raging sea lay at rest under his gaze, his disciples whispered, "What manner of man is this, that even the wind and the sea obey him?" (Mark 4:41).

Their question is our question. And the answer comes from Nicodemus, "We know that thou art a teacher come from God."

Who can help but say with the Nicene fathers: "I believe in . . . one Lord Jesus Christ, the only-begotten Son of God, Light of Light, very God of very God; begotten, not made, being of one substance with the Father, by whom all things were made."

Why, with all the studying, clawing, tearing, and hewing that Jesus' critics have done, would they not have exposed him centuries ago if he had been fake? To be sure. And the world would have cast him aside with the rest of the would-be messiahs of society.

But has it happened? Never. Rather, the more his enemies have assaulted him and the more his friends have studied him, questioned him, and searched him out, the brighter the Son of the Morning has shone. Could any man dream in his wildest imagination that this would be the case with a liar?

What did those who knew Jesus best say about him? John the Baptist, what do you say of the Carpenter of Nazareth? "Behold, the Lamb of God." Peter, Galilean fisherman and disciple of Jesus, what do you say? "Thou art the Christ, the Son of the living God." Thomas, you who doubted, what have you to say? "My Lord, and my God." And you, Pilate, you who tried him, what did you find? "I find no fault in the man." You also, John the beloved, you who were in the inner circle, what do you think of him? "In the beginning was the Word, and the Word was with God, and the Word was God. . . . And the Word was made flesh, and dwelt among us." Let the Roman soldier who guarded his cross speak. "Truly, this was the Son of God." Paul, persecutor of the church, what do you have to say concerning the one you so fiercely destroyed? "I count all things but loss for the excellency of the knowledge of Christ Jesus my Lord."

Now, let those who have been his enemies and his friends speak. Bob Ingersoll, noted atheist, said: "In using my speeches do not use any assault I may have made on Christ, which I foolishly made in my early life. . . . I believe Christ was the one perfect man."

While a prisoner in St. Helena, Napoleon said: "Alexander, Caesar, Charlemagne, and I, myself, have founded great empires; but upon what did these creations of our genius depend? Upon force. Jesus alone founded his empire upon love, and to this very day millions would die for Him. . . . I tell you, all these were men, and I am a man; none else is like Him; Jesus is more than man."

The Nazarene is so much a part of world history that Horace Bushnell said, "It were easier to untwist all the beams of light in the sky, separating and expunging one of the colors, than to get the character of Jesus, which is the real gospel, out of the world." Disraeli, the Jew and British prime minister, said, "Jesus has conquered Europe and has changed its name to Christendom." And Emerson reminds us that "the name of Jesus is not so much written as ploughed into the history of the world."

Theodore Parker raised the significant question: "Shall we be told such a man never lived; the whole story is a lie? . . . What man could have fabricated a Jesus? None but a Jesus."

Which of his disciples—fishermen and tax collectors—could have made up his sayings? Who invented his miracles? Why did the Jews kill him? What happened to his body? A thousand questions could be asked to show that those who deny the deity of Jesus are faced with a far greater dilemma than those of us who worship him as the only begotten Son of God.

And what shall we say of the Gospel records of Jesus' life? "Shall we," as Rousseau asked, "suppose the evangelical history a mere fiction? . . . The marks of its truth are so striking and inimitable, that the inventor would be a more astonishing character than the hero."

It is absolutely impossible to separate the Messiah from the Man and preserve any integrity of the four Gospels. To destroy him, you must destroy them. But to destroy them, you must explain them. Who conceived the person Jesus? Who thought his thoughts and portrayed his character?

John Stuart Mill is absolutely right when he says: "It is no use to say that Christ, as exhibited in the Gospels, is not historical." No honest thinker can read the evangelists without recognizing the Carpenter from Nazareth as Lord of all. For as Erasmus said, "Were we to have seen Him with our own eyes, we should not have so intimate a knowledge as they give us of Christ, speaking, healing, dying, rising again, as it were in our very presence."

It is not enough to read the sayings of noble men and great scholars. What men have thought about Jesus is significant, but not most significant. The real issue is, "What did Jesus believe about himself?" What claims did he make for his deity? Our court of final appeals for our faith must be the convictions and words of Jesus and not those of another.

H. G. Wells, eminent historian, declared that Jesus never made any claim to divinity. It is incredible that the author of the *Outline of History* would make so rash a statement. For nothing is clearer to a fair inquirer than the fact that Jesus believed himself to be the long-awaited Messiah and taught men so. Question his claims as the Messiah if you wish. But be honest enough not to question the fact that he made them. Only the blind and the prejudiced could miss that point in the Gospels.

Jesus' first and undisputed claim was made to the Samaritan woman by Jacob's well. His second claim was made to the man born blind. And his third was made to the high priest and the Sanhedrin. "But," someone may argue, "that is only three times." Once was enough to send him to the cross. Aren't three enough for us to believe?

Jesus wisely made few public claims to being the Messiah. For the messianic expectations of the Jews were weighted with hotheaded nationalism. They were too ready to proclaim the Messiah a political deliverer, take up the sword, and march on Rome. Jesus wanted to spare them this unnecessary suffering and death. (In the

thirty years before Herod the Great came to power, no less
than 150,000 Jews died in insurrections against Rome.)

And Christ had not come to deliver Israel from Rome but the
human race from sin—a deed exceedingly more important than
restoring the Davidic kingdom. But had he frequently and insis-
tently used the term *Messiah,* a messianic insurrection is certain
to have followed. For Judea was a revolutionary tinderbox, await-
ing only the spark of an unexpected deliverer.

The triumphal entry reveals that Jesus' fears were well founded.
The Jews believed that their hopes and aspirations were about to
be fulfilled. The Deliverer had come. Rome was about to be destroyed. The kingdom was about to be restored to Israel. They
cried, "Hosanna to the Son of David: Blessed is he that cometh
in the name of the Lord, Hosanna in the highest" (Matt. 21:9).
But a few days later, when their hopes had been shattered, they
shouted, "Crucify, crucify, crucify."

It is easy to see, therefore, why Jesus made the politically explosive and incendiary claim so sparingly. And for this same
reason, he urged his disciples to refrain from advertising him as
the Messiah. He even hushed the demons when they cried out,
calling him the Christ.

Jesus was no political deliverer. And he did not want the
people to cast him in that role. If they did, his spiritual message
would fall on deaf ears. But I remind you here that it was as the
Messiah that he was acclaimed and as the Messiah that he was
crucified.

Jesus frequently used two other messianic titles—the Son of
God and the Son of man. A third, the Son of David, he accepted
but never used himself. (The reason being, I think, because it was
even more politically explosive than "Messiah.")

Of all his titles, "Son of man" was Jesus' favorite. Eighty times
Jesus carefully and deliberately chose this messianic title for himself. Of course, it has been argued that this title does not neces-

sarily mean Jesus was claiming deity. It is true that *bar nasha* does mean simply man. But no argument can be built on that, for a text without a context is a pretext. And a doctrine built on a word meaning alone is ridiculous.

Jesus was speaking as the Messiah in fulfillment of Daniel 7: 13-14 when he used "Son of man." He was speaking of his divine and human nature, his shame and glory, his cross and crown, his borrowed bed and heavenly throne, his execution and triumph, his rejection by men and exaltation by God, his suffering servant-hood and reigning sonship.

Son of man was, by far, the most comprehensive title chosen by Jesus. And very likely it was freest of Jewish nationalistic expectations.

His second choice of titles was "Son of God." He applied this title to himself no less than twenty-five times in the Gospels. As Son of man, Jesus was blood kin of man; as the Son of God, he was (if you please) blood kin to God.

Look at the "I am" claims of Jesus: the Light of the world; the true Vine; the Bread of life; the Good Shepherd; the way, the truth, and the life; the door of the sheep; the resurrection and the life. Finally, he declared, "I AM." No greater claim to deity could be made. For here he identifies himself with the God of Sinai who revealed himself and his covenant name to Moses.

Look at the multitude of other claims Jesus made for himself—claims that would have been utter blasphemy had he not been divine. He claimed to be Lord of the sabbath; making himself equal with the God of creation. He claimed the right to forgive sin and that he himself was without sin. He claimed oneness with God, that he was the touchstone of all judgment, that he was the Savior of all men and without faith in him men would die in their sins. Among his claims were these: origin with God and return to God, the power to give eternal life, the power to raise the dead, the power to send the Spirit. Add to this the claim that everything that belonged to the Father belonged to him, that his teachings were not his own but were revealed from God, that he was greater than either Solomon or Jonah and you have either the babblings of a madman or the claims of the true Messenger from God.

Further, you will have to consider the fact that Jesus frequently accepted titles that would have been blasphemous if applied to anyone other than the Messiah. In at least two cases—the children in the Temple and the crowds at the triumphal entry—Jesus encouraged the use of these messianic titles even over the stern objections of the Pharisees. They were appalled that he would allow himself to be called: Lord, Master, Christ, Son of David, Son of God, the Holy One of God, the King of Israel. But Jesus quietly and properly accepted the acclamations of being just and true.

What do you think now of H. G. Wells's assertion that Jesus never claimed to be the Messiah? It is either a lie or ignorance. You may take your choice But as for me, I am persuaded that so eminent a historian could not have been ignorant of the Gospel records of the life of Jesus.

We may quibble over Jesus' claims about himself and his deity. But the Pharisees and scribes, the teachers of the law and Old Testament scholars made no mistake. They understood well what the Galilean was saying.

At first they were amazed, then horrified, and finally bitterly hostile. Often they were infuriated to the point of stoning him for the crime of blasphemy. And it was for this crime that they brought him at last to the cross.

When Jesus healed the lame man at Bethesda on the sabbath day, the Jews challenged his right to be working. Jesus replied, "My Father worketh hitherto, and I work." The Gospel writer notes that the Jews sought the more to kill him because he had not only broken the sabbath, but said also that God was his Father, making himself equal with God (John 5:17-18).

Jesus later laid claim to deity in words so plain and obnoxious to the Jews that they could bear it no longer. He said, "Verily, verily, I say to you, Before Abraham was, I am" (John 8:58). Jesus deliberately chose the sacred title of the covenant God of Israel—"I AM WHO I AM" (Ex. 3:14). The anger and frustration of the Jews blazed so hot that, contrary even to Roman law, they took up stones to stone him to death—the penalty prescribed for blasphemy (Lev. 24:16).

When Jesus made his fabulous claim, "I and my Father are one," the Jews again prepared to stone him. And Jesus challenged them, "Many good works have I shewed you from my Father; for which of those works do ye stone me?" The Jews replied, "For a good work we stone thee not; but for blasphemy; and because that thou, being a man, makest thyself God" (John 10:30, 32-33).

What was the question put to Jesus at his trial before Caiaphas? "Art thou the Christ, the Son of the Blessed?" Jesus replied without hesitation, "I am" (Mark 14:61-62). Horrified consternation seized the council. The high priest tore his clothes and cried, "What need we any further witnesses? Ye have heard the blasphemy: what think ye? And they all condemned him to be guilty of death" (Mark 14:63-64).

What were the slanderous taunts cast into his teeth at the cross? "Let Christ the King of Israel descend now from the cross, that we may see and believe" (Mark 15:32). "He trusted in God; let him deliver him now, if he will have him: for he said, I am the Son of God" (Matt. 27:43).

The Jews had a law, and by that law Jesus ought to die because he claimed to be the Son of God. They made no mistake when they brought the Nazarene to trial and execution. They had the right man—the Son of God.

What reasonable man, after hearing Jesus' claims and seeing the verification of those claims in words and deeds, can help but fall at his feet crying, "My Lord, and my God"?

A man who was born as Jesus was born, lived as Jesus lived, taught as Jesus taught, died as Jesus died, and came forth victorious over death and the grave can be no other than the Messenger come from God.

I fully agree with the young Japanese student who, one day after translating the Gospel of John, cried out, "Who is this man about whom I am reading—this Jesus? You call him a man, but he must be a God."

Christianity is Jesus Christ. Apart from him it is nothing. It centers in him and radiates from him. Separate the gospel from its incomparable Proclaimer and it dies immediately. Destroy the sonship of Jesus, and the Scriptures become a host of bold-faced fabrications.

But like a mountain punching its snow-covered peaks into the sun-drenched sky, Jesus stands above all criticism, bathed in the blazing light of the glory of God. He stands incarnate, living, crucified, risen, reigning, returning—preeminent above all teachers, prophets, kings, emperors, angels, and living creatures. He is the center of heaven's adoration, the light of the New Jerusalem, the sublimest truth of the Word of God. He is the object of every Christian's faith, and he shall one great day be the object of homage of all the ages.

Angels, all creation, and the redeemed shall join their voices in one mighty heavenly anthem of praise. Unbelievers, infidels, atheists, and ungodly men shall cry out with the dying sob of Julian the Apostate, "Thou hast conquered, O thou Galilean!"

2

ABBA, FATHER

Suppose for a moment you were God and wanted to tell men about yourself, how would you do it? Would you use great signs and miracles? How about prophets, angels, and special messengers? Would you use sacred writings, glorious creations, fiercely destructive powers? God used all of these. But when he wanted to speak plainly to us, he chose the way we understand best: another man.

God carved upon human flesh a true likeness of himself and called his name Jesus.

Christ carried the heart of God into the heat of battle for men's souls and inscribed his name forever upon the pages of human history. He became the chief architect of our knowledge of God, and showed us the Creator in terms we never knew until the Nazarene visited our planet. Since the day he walked on earth, God has no longer been a stranger to us; and we have no longer been strangers to him.

The Rosetta stone unlocked the secrets of the Egyptian hieroglyphics. What the Rosetta stone is to these ancient writings, is to the secrets of God. He opens up the divine mysteries to our souls. And when we search for a satisfying vision of God, our eyes turn immediately to him.

Henry Ward Beecher is right when he says that when we behold

Jesus Christ, we behold what God is in his inner disposition and soul. For God shines through the personality and in the face of the Savior. Other prophets and teachers have given us a partial vision of God, but Christ alone embodies the fullness of the Godhead. And in finding Christ, we find more than a way to God. We find God himself.

Guido's famous fresco, *The Aurora*, covers the lofty ceiling of the Rospigliosi Palace in Rome. Tourists looking up at the famous work find themselves growing dizzy and their necks getting stiff. When the figures blur, the visitors turn away. To solve the problem, the owner of the palace installed a large mirror near the floor. Now one may sit in comfort and enjoy the lovely fresco.

Like the Rospigliosi mirror, Christ reflects the true diety and heavenly beauty of God. What image could we have of God without the Son? True, we might get up an idea of our own; but how faulty that would be. We have no right to formulate our own foggy notions of God. Let us, rather, see and believe the truth about God. That truth is found in Jesus Christ.

A poor sick woman complained to her pastor: "Sir, I have no idea of God. I can form no thought of him. You talk to me about him, but I cannot get a single idea that seems to bring any comfort."

"But," he replied, "you know how to conceive of Jesus as a man, don't you?"

"Yes," she cried, "that gives me something to lay hold on. There I can rest."

Joseph Cook said, "My God is Jesus Christ, who came to pardon and save a world." And he is so right. For the Son is to the Father what the rays are to the sun. One cannot exist without the other. Eliminate the rays and the sun ceases to shine. Blot out the sun and the rays fail. Destroy the Son and the Father fades from the minds of men. Christ is the light by which all men may find their way to God.

The Son, though, is no dead moonlet, reflecting only the rays of

God's glory. He is no prism, bending the light of God to the eyes of men. He is the sun; he is the light. When we have seen him, we have seen the Father. I might further say that he who does not see the Father in the Son has shut his eyes to plain and revealed truth, and he will not see him at all.

Our world teems with attempts to paint and sculpt the Son of God. James Barry, the eighteenth-century artist, had long in his mind an idea of the face of Jesus. "It is here!" he would cry, striking his head with his hand. Leonardo da Vinci became so exhausted from attempting to create the face of Christ that he lay down his brush and left the painting headless.

A true image of God fails us. It escapes our imagination. We cannot grasp it. And no small wonder. No man has seen God at any time. All our true conceptions of the Father come from the Son. We are safe there, for we are looking at the Original from heaven, not a copy got upon earth.

Did this Jesus have something unique to say about God? If so, what was it? Our answer comes in one single stroke: Father. Jesus knew the Eternal, Almighty, Sovereign, Jehovah God as his Father; and he taught us that we, too, may know him as our Father.

Us, children of God! I stagger at the thought. "Is it true?" I ask. Can it ever be true that the Lord God of Sinai, the Creator of the ends of the earth, the God of destruction and fire, will ever be a Father to mortal men?

Yes, it is true. Why do I say so? Because Jesus said so. What's more, he so lived that we could know he spoke the truth. What we see in him—living, speaking, working, dying—impresses us with the indisputable fact that God was, indeed, his Father; and he will be our's also.

The presence of the stars is not proved by astronomy. The changing seasons are not proved by a calendar. The shining of the stars prove their presence. Falling rain and green twigs tell us that winter is passing and spring is on its way.

Just so, the unique God-consciousness of Jesus is not verified by argument, labored examinations, and certificates of his deity. The fragrance of God in his life, the wisdom of God upon his lips, the light of God in his face, the touch of God in his hands, and the testimony of God in his soul are the things that convince us. His perfect identity with the Father and total submission to his will impress us more than all his teachings. For we still prefer an example above words.

George Bernard Shaw said, "What a man believes may be ascertained not from his creed, but from the assumptions on which he habitually acts."

Behind the words of Jesus about the Father lies the mind and life of the Son, a man and life committed to one unconquerable conviction—that God was his Father in a way that he was Father to no other.

"All things are delivered unto me of my Father," said Jesus, "and no man knoweth the Son, but the Father; neither knoweth any man the Father, save the Son, and he to whomsoever the Son will reveal him" (Matt. 11:27).

To be sure, "The greatest spiritual fact that has ever emerged in the long history of the human race is Jesus of Nazareth's consciousness of God," said James Alexander Robertson.

Others may be sons of God by faith in the Son of God. But Jesus alone can claim unique sonship. No other one can claim, and verify his claim, that he bears the same intimate relationship to the Father that Jesus bore.

The Savior never used "our Father" except in teaching his disciples to pray. He always spoke of "my Father" or "the Father." He never made the mistake of equating our sonship with his sonship.

Jesus was "in the bosom of the Father" (John 1:18). To be in the bosom of the Father was to be as close as possible to him.

It was the phrase used of a Jewish child nestling in its mother's arms or of a wife held close to her husband. By this saying, John assured us that Jesus lived next to the very heart of God.

When the Savior went into Gethsemane and the gaunt shadow of the cross fell across his face, he cried out to his Father. When the bitter cup of sin touched his lips, he fled to his Father. When the nails tore his hands and his feet and the sword pierced his side, he pressed close to his Father's side.

Hear Jesus pray in those dark hours: "Abba, Father" (Mark 14:36). Ah, what a prayer! "Abba" is the Aramic word that Jesus always used in speaking to his Father. It was the usual word a Jewish child of Jesus' day would use in speaking to his daddy. Perhaps it would be best to translate the word just that—"Abba, Daddy, Father."

Do you see how intimate Jesus was with God? Do you see how the anguish of Gethsemane, the encircling hate of the world, and the approaching cross pressed the Son to the heart of the One he knew and loved best?

But that is not all. At his death, he prayed the prayer that every Jewish child learned: "Into thy hands I commend my spirit (Luke 23:46). (It was something of a "Now I lay me down to sleep" prayer.) But Jesus added an infinitely important dimension. What was it? "Father" was what the Son of God added, and it completely transformed this familiar child's prayer.

This epitaph is carved on a child's gravestone in a churchyard in England: "Freddy! . . . Yes, Father." How like the final whisper of Jesus from the cross!

A young army officer was fatally wounded in the jungles of South Vietnam. Just before his radio went dead, he began babbling about home and began calling his mother and father.

From the muddy rice paddies of the Orient, death drove his soul across the Pacific to the living room of his home. And from the gnarled olive trees and stony ground of Gethsemane, the heart

of Jesus fled across space to the One dearest to him. "Abba,
Father." Dear God, what a plea. It is hardly reasonable that
mortal men should have heard it.

Had this cry come from any other lips, men would have been
amazed. "Incredible," we would have cried. But how perfectly
natural it sounds coming from Jesus.

Jesus lived in the serene confidence that "thou hearest me always" (John 11:42). His communion with the Father was complete, totally uninterrupted. Never a cloud or a shadow drifted
between them. There were no short circuits, no broken connec-
tions. Never a bit of rust of neglect or corrosion of sin collected
to interrupt their union.

Heaven bent low over the earth while Christ walked here. Time
and distance could not separate the Father from his Son.

No man ever prayed like Jesus prayed. He prayed late at night
and early in the morning. He sought the desert places, the moun-
tains, and the solitary refuge; but he also could be alone with his
Father in a crowd.

He prayed when tempted, criticized, wearied, perplexed, praised,
and crucified. He made no important decisions without the coun-
sel of the Father.

Christ was praying when the Spirit descended upon him. He
prayed when the tempter stood astride his pathway and challenged
his right to his sonship. When great crowds thronged him, appeal-
ing to him to be their king, Jesus prayed.

He prayed when the religious leaders from Jerusalem dogged his
footsteps, carping, nagging, sowing seeds of hate and distrust.
Weary with their petty picking, the Nazarene sought the solace of
his Father's face.

When the hour came to choose his disciples, Jesus talked it over
with his Father. He had so much to consider: Judas, the betrayer;
Simon, the reed; Thomas, the doubter. Violent death would come
most of these men because of their devotion to him.

As he began the last year of his ministry and the swirling waters of human sin washed ever closer, Jesus frequently went alone to pray. When the disciples returned from their missionary journey with their victorious report, our Lord spoke to his Father about it. At the graveside of Lazarus, Jesus talked to his Father about the danger the miracle would hold for Lazarus as well as for himself. At the visit of the Greeks, in the upper room, and in Gethsemane, Jesus communed with God.

He spent his last few moments in the garden alone with his Father. Before the Jewish mob, the traitor, and the Roman soldiers came, Jesus wanted to talk everything over with him.

What communion with God, what agony of prayer transpired in that garden! The nightmare of the next day pressed upon him. He struggled alone with the bitter cup. Human strength failed. Spiritual and mental agony seared his soul. Sweat came like blood through his skin. Tension tore at his soul.

Did the Father stand idly by while his Son suffered? Not at all. He sent heavenly messengers down to minister to his only begotten.

Deep silence hung over heaven. A hush fell on the holy place of God. Quiet moved across God's throne as Jesus lay in deep communion with his Father.

His final words from the cross were his childhood prayer, "Father, into thy hands I commend my spirit." Then he fled away back into the bosom of God.

Never at any time did Jesus act independently of his Father. He shared all his thoughts, judgments, and plans with him. What he saw the Father do, he did. His Father had given him power to raise the dead, do miracles, and judge the world. He had come in his Father's name, and bore the seal of his Father's approval. His Father loved him and was constantly with him. His words were the words of his Father. Heaven was his Father's house, and he had sole access to the door.

All that he possessed had been given him by his Father. He who

had seen the Son had seen the Father. He who loved the Son and
honored him, loved and honored the Father also. Whoever hated
the Son, hated also the Father. Whoever knew and received the
Son, knew and received the Father, too. He came from the Father
and returned to him. He and the Father were one.

I find it exciting that the first recorded words of Jesus were,
"I must be about my Father's business" (Luke 2:49). Here at the
early age of twelve, Jesus portrayed a special awareness of God.
He was even a bit perturbed that Mary and Joseph had thrashed
about the empty alleys and places of play. Did they not know
that his Father's affairs had first claim upon him?

These words were spoken in his Father's house. He stood among
scribes and Pharisees who would not so much as pronounce the
name of Jehovah aloud. But here was Jesus calling him "Father"
in the most familiar tones.

Jesus spoke of God being his Father one hundred and forty-six
times in the Gospels. One hundred and thirteen of them are in
the Gospel of John. How fitting it is that John should write most
conclusively of Jesus' sonship. He was the disciple whom Jesus
loved, and a member of the inner circle. He recognized Jesus
first as the Messiah; he believed in him most thoroughly; and
leaned on his bosom at the Last Supper. The solitary flower
of the God-consciousness of Jesus that blooms here and there
in the other Gospels becomes a bed of fragrant blossoms in John.

Jesus lived in God, and he lived God out in the stream of human
experience. His meat and drink was to do the will of his Father.
"Not my will, but thine be done" was the supreme commitment
of his life. And that commitment made even the horrors of the
cross a "joy set before him."

Jesus was not without a will. He had one of his own. This had
been given to him by his Father. And in the free exercise of his
will, he chose to live in total submission to the will of his Father.
But isn't that what we would expect of him? Isn't it as much a

part of his divinity as are his miracles and teachings?

One of the Space Age's most ingenious devices is the star tracker. Space scientists install this delicate instrument in huge rockets before launch. Star tracker is preset to certain selected stars of known magnitude and location. By maintaining a constant "fix" on those selected stars, star tracker keeps the earth-orbiting satellite precisely on its preplanned flight path.

The will of God was Jesus' star tracker. And in spite of all Satan's temptations that tried to tear him away from his mission, the will of God kept the Son on his course toward the cross.

The Gospels paint the portrait of one who delighted to do his Father's will. Every action, every step was a commitment of obedience. In his baptism, he committed himself to the ministry God had given him. The Jordan was to Jesus what the Rubicon was to Caesar. When he stepped into those rushing waters, the die was cast. There was no turning back. The Son of God was on his way to Calvary.

At a word he could have turned from the cross and returned to the comfort of his Father's throne. In judgment, he could have smitten the earth with a curse. Yet he thirsted, wept, grieved, suffered, and died in obedience to his Father's will.

From a cow stall in Bethlehem through a carpenter shop in Nazareth, and finally to Calvary, the will of the Father led the Savior. And his murmurless going bears mute testimony to his perfect sonship.

Someone asked General Stonewall Jackson, "Could you go to Africa without a murmur if God called you?" He replied, "Sir, I could go without my hat."

In Gethsemane's silence Christ's heart could hear, "Drink this cup. It is your Father's will." His Father's hand held the cup of human sin to his lips. And that touch made the gall of wickedness tolerable.

There is a lovely legend that Nimrod once took Abraham and

threw him into a furnace of fire because he would not worship his idols. But God promptly changed the bed of coals to a bed of flowers. And I have no doubt that the bitterest anguish of Jesus' life was sweetened by his Father's will.

The wealth of the world and the regalia of heaven were his. Yet "he humbled himself, and become obedient unto death, even the death of the cross" (Phil. 2:8). Stars, garters, crowns, and earthly glory held no charm for Jesus. He would not so much as turn a stone to bread to satisfy his hunger. Neither would he cast himself down from the rampart of the Temple to gain glory. He opened not his mouth in his own defense. Why? Because he was certain that all that was happening to him was his Father's will.

In the midst of deceit and betrayal, Jesus had perfect composure. In the face of desertion by his disciples, he was perfectly steadfast. He faced the might of imperial Rome without shrinking. And in the presence of total rejection by Israel, he was kept in perfect peace.

"There is no disappointment," said Frederick Faber, nineteenth-century priest and writer, "to those whose wills are buried in the will of God."

Jesus endured without murmuring, questioning, doubting, or striking back. He sought no further reward than to know that he was pleasing his heavenly Father.

When sorrow tore at Jesus' heart, when his family doubted his sanity, when his enemies condemned him, and when it seemed that heaven lifted not a finger to help, did he draw back? No. Jesus trusted in the gracious will of God, and that trust softened the grimness of the hour.

When the chill of death stole over his soul, did he object? Not at all. When heaven was silent and his cry seemed to fall on deaf ears, did he have any misgivings? He did not. Rather, he cried, "What shall I say? Father, save me from this hour: but for this cause came I unto this hour" (John 12:27).

Such a one was Jesus, God's perfect Son. Though he were equal with God, he was totally dependent on him. Though he possessed Spirit without measure, yet he prayed for strength and guidance.

Noah was commended because "he pleased God" (Heb. 11:5). But it was reserved for Jesus to please God perfectly. His every act was signed with this postscript: "If God wills."

Jesus! Who is this one who prayed so earnestly, "Abba, Father"? He is the perfect image of the invisible God, the perfect revelation of the Father.

"If Christ be not God," Beecher said, "then to worship him is idolatry, and the Father has deluded and deceived the world." Then Beecher added, "O Lord Jesus! My heart cries out from its depth that thou art very God."

3

CHAMPION OF THE PEOPLE

An ancient Eastern legend tells of Jesus arriving late one evening at the city of Nazareth. He sent his disciples ahead to prepare supper while he himself walked about the streets.

As Jesus drew near the marketplace, he saw a crowd looking at something on the ground. He walked up to see what it was and discovered that it was a dead dog with a rope tied around its neck. The creature had been dragged through the dirt and stones of the street. It was broken and torn and filthy. Bystanders looked at it with disgust.

"Faugh!" they cried, stopping their noses. "It pollutes the air." "How long," said one, "shall this foul beast offend our sight?" "Look at his torn hide," said another. "You could not even cut a shoe out of it." "And his ears," cried a third, "all ripped and bleeding." "No doubt," they all agreed, "he was hanged for thieving."

Jesus heard them. And looking with compassion on the dead creature, he said, "Pearls do not equal to the whiteness of his teeth."

The people turned in amazement and cried: "Who is this? This must be Jesus of Nazareth, for only he could find something to pity and approve in a dead dog." Being ashamed, they bowed their heads before him, and each went on his way.

We may doubt the legend, but we cannot deny its moral, for Jesus saw the good in all men. He saw the gold in the masses of forgotten people, and he sought it with compassion and persistence.

The psalmist raised the question, "What is man, that thou art mindful of him?" (Ps. 8:4). Is he saint or sinner, killer or creator of life, handiwork of creation or product of evolution, child of God or son of Satan? We may suspect that he is some of all of it. But God comes at us with the real answer: Man is God's creation; made in the image of God and made only a little lower than God. Though he is stained with sin and the image of God is effaced, he is worth saving.

This speck of dust called man creeps around on a ball of dirt, hanging in the vastness of God's universe. Yet he is the special object of God's love and attention. He is worth to God not only more than the sparrows but all of his creation as well. It was for man, and for man alone, that the Son of God came, suffered, and died.

Jesus believed in men. He was a people person. What sin had destroyed, his grace could restore. For that reason he set out on his long journey from his throne to his cross. He came to save men from their sins and to restore their sonship to God. He came to recreate man—plain, simple, insignificant man; holes in punch cards, digits in computers, faceless souls in the sea of society.

What is man? He is a priceless possession in God's sight. He is worth the life of God's Son. Why, then, do we ignore Christ and destroy the human being he came to save? Why do we prostitute the souls of the children of God to industrial production and sacrifice them to the gods of technology? Isn't this a sign of sin's deepest stain within our souls? Why else would we hate and twist and waste the very object of God's deepest love?

There is a question far more important than "What is man?" It is this: "What can man become?" For our answer, let's look to Jesus. For the heights to which any man may go can be found only in him.

He was born in a cow stable in an out-of-the-way village in a province ruled by imperial Rome. He grew up in a carpenter shop in the city of Nazareth in the hill country of Galilee. He preached three years. He was often unbefriended and had little money. He was called "beside himself" by his family, a heretic and blasphemer by Judaism, a traitor to his nation. He was executed as a felon by Rome, and the only one to honor him in death was a murderer. Yet after two thousand years his name is known to people all over the world.

Let none of us, therefore, be found saying "I can't." For Jesus, who was bone of our bone and flesh of our flesh, gave us a living demonstration that we can. He brought us hope for the future and gave us purpose for living. Because he was good, gentle, kind, and just, the Son of man convinced us that a better life is possible for us all. He gave us something more than teeth-gritting determination to hold onto. He gives us more than the power to bear our lot until death mercifully sets us free.

Every living person can look into the face of Christ and take hope. For he provides the model and the opportunity for human fulfillment. He restores our humanity and gives us back our spark of divinity. He lifts us out of our helplessness and despair. He heals our hurts and relieves the oppression of our sins.

When Jesus stepped upon the pages of history, human life was worth little. Women, children, slaves, the sick, and the forgotten people were worth nothing. They were zeroes, dispensable items on the agenda of the Caesars.

High taxes, oppression, restriction of freedom, forced labor, depressed living standards, and the decayed status of the human being combined to make life intolerable. The shame and humiliation of paying tribute to Rome added to the burden. Free corn and circuses were small compensation for the sacrifice of human dignity.

The "haves" stood on the necks of the "have-nots." Rome sacrificed humans to hungry lions and cheered as the bloody beasts devoured their mangled bodies. In ruthless contempt for human life, unwanted babies were cast out like dogs to die in sewers and gutters.

An Egyptian of the first century wrote his pregnant wife in Rome: "I pray and beseech you, take care of the little child. . . . If you are delivered, if it was a male; let it live, if it was a female, cast it out."

Hebrew men recited a favorite prayer that thanked God they had not been born women.

Into this sort of world, degraded by Rome and disillusioned with false messiahs, Jesus came. He came possessed with the revolutionary idea that all human life was sacred before God. He preached a "whosoever" gospel—an idea totally foreign to his day, and almost to ours.

In three and a half years, Jesus revolutionized the thinking of the world about human life. And since his visit to our planet, life has been a little better and human rights a little surer.

A remarkable testimony to his divinity, wouldn't you say?

A boy said to his mother as she told him the gospel story: "Mother, I don't see the great merit in Christ dying for us. If I could save a dozen men by dying for them, I think I would." His mother wisely replied: "But suppose they were grasshoppers? Would you die for them?" The boy thought for a minute and said, "I don't know for sure about grasshoppers. They are a pretty clever bunch. But if they were mosquitoes, I think I'd just let them go and die."

What did Jesus say about those for whom he died? "For the Son of man is come to save that which was lost" (Matt. 18:11). He spent his brief life opening the eyes of the blind, making the lame walk, healing the brokenhearted, setting at liberty the captives, and preaching the acceptable year of the Lord (see Luke 4:18-19).

Jesus worked among the people who needed him and wanted him. There was the widow of Nain, weeping over her dead son; Mary and Martha of Bethany, sorrowing over their dead brother; Jairus, grieving over his dying daughter.

Christ walked through the porches of Bethesda until he found the most hopeless case of all, and sent him home sound and well. A little woman with an issue of blood crept up behind the Savior and was healed. He stopped an argument between his disciples and healed the man born blind. He waited on a crowded road to heal the eyes of a blind beggar.

By the seaside, he taught the people the love of God. In the wilderness, he fed the hungry multitudes. Lepers felt his tender touch. Children danced around him, singing his praises. Babies nestled in his tender arms. Fishermen found in him a compatriot. Zacchaeus, Levi, and other tax gatherers discovered a friend. Harlots found merciful forgiveness for their sins and restoration of their self-respect. Truly, Christ got down on our level except for our sins.

On the birthday of Robert Stephenson, a large crowd gathered in New Castle. They covered the town with grand colors and vast banners in honor of the distinguished engineer. Among the many processions, there was a band of peasants from Stephenson's home village. They carried a small banner bearing this slogan, "He Was One of Us."

Of all the titles and crowns that men may heap upon the Savior, let none be more prominent than this: He was one of us. And may we of the earth, on the Great Day of God, politely ask angels and living creatures to stand aside while we raise above all thrones and dominions our banner: "He Was One of Us."

Jesus' life is summed up in these words, "He went about doing good." He went about forgiving the guilty and sorrowing over the rebellious. He called the weary and those who were heavy laden to himself and lifted up the fallen.

But we are different. The German poet, Hienrich Heine, probably expressed our own secret feelings when he said: "I, too, might have died for men if I had not the suspicion that they were not worth it." And very likely the reason Jesus *did* die for us is that he believed we *were* worth it.

On one of his many tours of the British Empire, the Prince of Wales stopped off in India. Everything was ready for the royal welcome. The upper castes greeted the prince with great pomp and ceremony. But barriers had been erected along the stretch to keep back the outcastes. Seeing this poor, wretched troop gathered behind the barricades, the Prince of Wales ordered the barriers removed. To the astonishment of the upper castes, he plunged into this seething mass of unwanted humanity, shaking hands and greeting beggars, laborers, and untouchables.

A few years later the Prince returned to India. He was again greeting by the same scene. But this time something had changed. There were no barriers. And the ragtag band that lined the streets carried a banner that read "The Prince of the Outcastes."

Who deserves this title more than Jesus? He was the Messiah of the man-on-the-street. A greater commoner never lived. His sympathies lay with the poor, the working classes, and the irreligious. He made a Galilean fishing village his headquarters and called common men to be his disciples. He often said: "I will have mercy, and not sacrifice" (Matt. 9:13).

Even his triumphal entry was a "poor man's procession." Galilean hillbillies threw their coarse coats on the ground for a carpet. His white charger was a donkey. And his martial music was the hoarse shouts of the multitudes who hailed him as their hero.

When he preached, the common folk knew immediately that he was one of them and heard him gladly. Jesus had what Bonhoeffer called a "strange brotherhood with the irreligious."

Judaism gave the edge to the wealthy. But Jesus identified himself with the life struggle of the average person and sympathized with the underdog. To him, the unchurched were not an ignorant mob accursed from God to be cold-shouldered by organized religion.

The Savior walked where they walked and sat where they sat. He was a member of a minority group and grew up feeling the pinch of poverty. His stories betray the fact that he knew the value of two mites, a single lost coin, and a lost sheep.

But there is more to the mind of Christ toward men than his common brotherhood. He did not simply reflect his identification with the life experiences of the poor He was more than a child of his time. Jesus revealed the loving concern of God for all men, especially the unloved.

He told us that God's sun shines and his rain falls on the just and the unjust. God's blessings belong to the lofty pine and the lowly bramble. Both the gorgeous rose and the wild violet hold title to them. And there is no creature so poor or so low that he may not look up into the face of God and say, "Father."

Disease, deformity, and poverty could not erase Jesus' sense of the worth of a human being. As someone has said: "The deeper our insight into human destiny becomes, the more sacred does every individual human being seem to us." But the twentieth century has a cold, calculating attitude toward life. Affluence, greed, and the drive for more and more production are creating a callous indifference toward the unfit, the unwanted, and the unborn. We are sacrificing human life on the altar of progress. Real estate, power, and position are the things that count. People are losing out to machines.

And unless we soon return to Christ's love and regard for human life, it is anybody's guess who will be next. Today it is the unborn. Tomorrow it will be the aged, the defective, and the infirm.

Henry C. King said that the principle of reverence for personality is the ruling principle in ethics, and in religion. I might add, "in honorable human society as well."

Jesus labored to save what the world had cast aside as worthless. He saw the unfortunate, the despised, and the neglected as sheep having no shepherd. Even the hated half-breeds of Samaria found a friend in him. How striking and how well earned was the slur, "Why eateth your Master with publicans and sinners" (Matt 9:11). (A badge of honor, wouldn't you say?)

Christ commended a Roman soldier for his faith and healed a lunatic in a graveyard. He welcomed Gentiles from the east and from the west into the banquet halls of the kingdom with Abraham, Isaac, and Jacob. He preached to Greeks and Idumaeans, people from beyond Jordan, and those from the neighborhoods of Tyre and Sidon. He reminded the Jews that Elijah found shelter with a Gentile woman and that Elisha had healed only one leper, a Syrian army officer.

The heroes of his parables were the despised Samaritans. The chief characters of his gospel were publicans, soldiers, harlots, Galileans, and fishermen. He saw in the village of Sychar a field white unto harvest. And he often found himself dining with tax collectors and their cronies. He even dared suggest to the wealthy Pharisees that they invite to their banquets the cripples, the vagrants, and the blind rather than the important people about town.

Christ accepted the courtesies of a wayward woman, and he stopped dying long enough to save a thief. He traveled through Samaria to redeem a sinful woman, and he healed a Syrophenician girl near Tyre and Sidon. Even the stubborn, dishonest religious leaders came in for their share of compassion. They joined hands with the Romans to make common cause against the Savior. Yet he wept over their senseless rejection of him and his message.

In Jesus' day jails were for the poor. The upper classes were hedged about with honor while the lower classes were treated as "things." The powerless received no justice in the courts, and punishment was reserved for the disinherited.

Jesus was different. He saw beneath the commonplace, the selfish, the sordid, the repulsive externals of life. To him, men were never a means to an end. They were not a labor force or a business world. They were children of God.

Christ never used his vast powers for show or self-benefit. He placed himself and all his might sqarely alongside human need. Where there was suffering, he brought comfort. Where there was sin, he brought forgiveness. Where there was loneliness, he brought cheer. Where there was disease, he brought healing. Where there was despair, he brought hope. Where there was death, he brought life.

Jesus did not worry about consequences. He befriended Mary of Magdala without fearing the ugly insinuations that were bound to follow. He did not fear even to touch lepers. Repulsive to look at, repugnant to touch, and feared because of infection, lepers were sentenced to live in waste places and beg. They were stoned if they attempted to come where other people lived. But Jesus freely loved and freely healed people such as these.

The Savior flabbergasted the Pharisees by his conduct. He rejected their religious conventions and refused to live behind their sanctified fences. He did not waste his time backslapping the "right" people and mollycoddling the well-to-do. Rather he went out and lived among those he had come to save.

To Jesus, there were no barriers, no super races, and no untouchables. He forbade the strong to trample the weak. Instead of eliminating the unfit, he proposed to make them whole. Christ saw people—plain honest-to-goodness people with common strengths and weaknesses, fear and hopes, sins and merits.

But how often do those who need us most receive only a nod or even a rebuke? They come to us for help, but find a cold heart, a suspicious mind, and an unforgiving spirit.

Henry Ward Beecher tells of a man who was arrested for counterfeiting. He went to prison, served his time, and returned to New York. The man did not try to hide his crime; he was willing to take any job offered him. He went first to his old friends. They eyed him with suspicion and acted as if he had some loathsome disease. Everybody suspected him. Nobody trusted him.

After a year of this, he went to Beecher and told his story. Then he added: "Mr. Beecher, I receive sympathy from none but the worst folks. I receive nothing but unkindness from the best folks. What am I going to do?"

If we would be Christians, we can no longer harbor doubts and hatred of any man. Our churches cannot be holdouts of prejudice and indifference.

For the church sinks to no greater depths than when she condones racism and human exploitation in the name of God. She denies her birthright when she, out of fear of the consequences, fails to have the mind of Christ toward all people. No man, no church can pray "Our Father" and exclude any person without being a denial of the life and teachings of Jesus.

The only valid question then for the church to ask herself is: Dare we live by the teachings and example of Jesus? Dare we really be Christians? Unless we do, there is no need to go further. The one unanswerable argument for Christianity is a *real* Christian.

And what is it to be a Christian? Nothing less than to think like Jesus thought and act like Jesus acted. It is to go out where people live and work and die; to touch the raw edges of their lives and by that touch bring hope and healing.

Walter Rauschenbusch spoke the truth when he said: "A man is a Christian in the degree in which he shares the spirit and consciousness of Jesus Christ, concerning God as Jesus knew him and seeing human life as Jesus realized it."

It is with us as it was with the Savior: The works that we do in our Father's name, they bear witness of us (John 5:36).

But the church has largely forsaken the mind of Christ toward men. His plans, his programs for redeeming men and lifting up the fallen have been cast aside in favor of schemes for strengthening organized religion. We should not be surprised that the common man does not feel the church is for him.

Human selfishness and firmly entrenched social customs have been slow to yield to the thought of Jesus. The rich and the powerful have not readily accepted his ideas as practical. The teachings of Christ must take a firmer hold of us all. For without his belief in the worth of the individual, social justice will disappear, philanthropy will dry up, and democratic institutions will vanish. The hope for lifting up the fallen and redeeming the lost will be gone. Civil liberties will be a relic of the past, and the earth will be plunged deeper into the night of barbarism and hate.

Christ and his mission have redeemed many cultures from their darkness and softened their callousness toward women, children, and the disinherited. Christ has brought a new warmth and regard for human life and eased the lot of a very great many.

But Jesus' first principle of life, "Thou shalt love," must be put into practice in the business houses, homes, communities, and churches of our world. Tolerance and brotherhood must take the place of exclusiveness and snobbery. Who are the people best qualified to do this? Those who profess to be children of God and believers in Christ's teachings, that is who. What institution is best suited to do this? The church.

Unless we soon set to work at this task, unless there is a rebirth of the attitude of Christ toward all men, we may yet blow ourselves off this ball of dirt.

If we do decide, however, to follow Jesus' teachings, we will soon find ourselves as the helpers of men. We will share the lives of those who suffer, sin, and die. And we may discover the giant shadow of the cross falling across our pathway.

4

THE SIN QUESTION

He who writes for long about Jesus without mentioning the Savior's attitude toward the sinful and erring misses the most significant point in the personality of the Son of God. For nothing else so sets the Nazarene apart as unique Man among men.

Pharisaism sat as a harsh and unyielding judge of sinners. Its God was not in the business of saving the wayward but of destroying them.

Christ stood in stark contrast to his native religion. The God he brought to us yearned for the lost, filled his banquet halls with vagrants and cripples, and cast out the self-righteous folk. And that gracious attitude of God toward sinners is, more than anything else, Jesus' special gift to our world.

May it please God to grant to his church today Christ's unquenchable love for the sinner, his forgiving spirit for the immoral, and his yearning for the lost. Then we might, indeed, be a true reflection of the Savior to a sinful world; for a man's kinship to Jesus can be better discerned by his attitude toward sin than by anything else he does or says.

I read of a pilgrim who arrived at the gates of heaven. He stood in the outer courts of the city and watched as a glorious host came marching up, clad in shimmering white. They were singing the sweetest hymns and bearing banners of victory.

As they passed through the gates and vanished out of sight, he asked, "Who are they?"

"They are the grand fellowship of the prophets who have gone to be with God," replied the keeper of the gate.

"Ah," said he, "I am not one of them and never shall be. I cannot enter here."

Soon another band came, more glorious and lovely in appearance. They marched triumphantly, clothed in their white robes. As they entered the portals of heaven, great shouts of welcome rose from within the walls.

"And who are these?" he asked.

"These are the faithful fellowship of the apostles," answered the gatekeeper.

With a drooping heart, he sighed: "Neither do I belong with these. I cannot enter here."

Still he lingered in hopes that perchance he might yet go in. But the next throng did not encourage him either, for they were the noble army of martyrs. He could not enter with them or wave their palm branches of victory.

He waited still, but the next group to come was the company of godly ministers and missionaries of the church. He stood and watched them disapper within the city walls to the sound of shouts and triumphal hymns.

At last, as he began to walk away, he saw a host larger than all the rest, marching and singing with the greatest melody and joy. In front walked the woman taken in adultery. The thief who died on the cross marched beside her. And there was Zacchaeus, the publican, the Samaritan woman, and Mary of Magdala.

As he surveyed the motley crowd, he thought, "There will be no shouting in heaven if these enter." But to his astonishment, it seemed as if all heaven vibrated with shouts as they passed within the gates.

"And who are these?" he asked.

The guardian angel said, "These are they that are mighty sinners, saved by mighty grace."

He leaped for joy. "Blessed be God," he cried. "I can go in with them."

The Reverend John Brown of Haddington, Scotland, said, "It has been my comfort these twenty years, that not only sensible sinners, but the most stupid, are made welcome to believe in Christ." For the Savior did, while on this earth, most graciously welcome the soiled and the sinful. And we have no reason to think he has ever changed his mind.

Jesus said little about sin; especially the sins we major on. He dealt with only five moral offenders in whose cases he pointedly referred to their sins. Even in these he spoke in forgiveness and admonition, not in condemnation.

But Christ was not soft on sin or casual in his treatment of human guilt. He was no flabby sentimentalist. Neither did he give any quarter to the hardhearted and unrepentant. Even the humble and submissive he told to "go, and sin no more" (John 8:11).

Our Lord would have agreed with the old-time Methodists who said, "We know no gospel without salvation from sin." Remember how, in the case of the palsied man, he put forgiveness ahead of healing? Here is an undeniable witness that Jesus regarded sin as a worse enemy than palsy, and the soul more important than the body.

No man knew sin better than Jesus. No one was more revolted by its ominous power. Yet he dealt with sinners in gentle forbearance. The weakest, sin-stained soul felt completely comfortable in his presence. The bruised reed he did not break, and the smoking flax he did not quench. He spent his life, both in living and in dying, redeeming those who would be redeemed and weeping over those who would not.

The Prince of Wales once asked Lady Charlotte, "Where is My

Lady Huntingdon, that she is so seldom here.?" "I suppose," snapped the fashionable lady, "she is out praying with her beggars."

Jesus had that sort of reputation. And he earned it well. Publicans and harlots flocked around him. Town strumpets wet his feet with their tears. Tax collectors climbed trees to catch a glimpse of him. Redeemed sinners poured precious ointment over his head. And a dying criminal found comfort in his presence.

I find it remarkable that the only sinless Man who ever lived had the deepest compassion for sinners of any man who ever lived. Jesus wore a halo of pure heavenly holiness. But he wore it with such grace that the vilest of sinners looked up to him as their champion. No religious exclusiveness flowed in his veins. He did not fear these moral lepers. He moved among them like the sun shining in darkness, and his warmth was a welcome change to the frigid light of Pharisaism.

Jesus loved and respected these outcasts. He wanted to be with them, and they knew it. He did not look upon them with an air of critical condemnation. To Jesus, they were people worthy of his attention. And this sense of brotherhood drew them to him.

When criticized for his liberal attitude toward sinners, the Savior's only defense was: "They that be whole need not a physician, but they that are sick. . . . I am not come to call the righteous, but sinners to repentance" (Matt. 9:12-13).

Look how the Savior handled the worst moral offenders that came to his attention.

There was the sinner woman that Jesus met by Jacob's well (John 4:1-42). The Master rested in the cool shade while his disciples went to buy food. He watched the heat devils dance on the dirt road to Sychar. Slowly a lonely figure dragged in sight around the bend. It was a woman; a woman trudging along, burdened by her sin and rejction as well as by her water-pot. She came alone at an unusual hour. At noon she came, hoping no one would be at the well. For the Samaritan woman was tired of the digs and the stares of the "ladies" of Sychar.

But she was in for a surprise. There beside the well sat a Jew. She glanced at him and went on about her business of drawing water. Up from the well came the bag of cool, fresh water. She filled her waterpot, got herself a drink, and turned to go.

The Stranger had been watching her all the time. Suddenly he spoke, "Give me a drink." Stunned with surprise, she whirled around and snapped back, "How is it that you, a Jew, would ask a drink from me, a Samaritan woman?"

In a few moments the conversation shifted. Her quips stopped. Her questions fell silent. The Stranger had struck home to her need.

"Go, call your husband, and come here," he said.

"I have no husband," she replied.

Jesus had hit a raw nerve. But he did it with such gentleness that she did not resent it. Her haughtiness left her. Her immoral life swam before her eyes. And she unburdened her soul to the Savior.

Jesus brought her abruptly but graciously face to face with her sin. He awakened in her a sleeping desire to be free from her guilt and to be a better person. She longed to be a human being again, and he was just the one to help.

Kindly but firmly Jesus lay bare her sordid past. She was not bitter about it though, for he did it to help, not to criticize and condemn. She knew he had not asked these personal questions because he enjoyed a bit of raw gossip or because he wanted to see her squirm. His voice had a sympathetic tone, and his eyes held no threat or accusation. Gently Jesus brought her to salvation.

Jesus had risked his good name by doing so. It was a disgrace for a rabbi to be seen talking to a woman, even his wife, in public. And here was Jesus not only talking to a woman, but a Samaritan woman with a questionable reputation. No ordinary Jew would have done that. The rabbis would not have passed so much as a word of greeting. But the Savior spent several minutes in conversation with her. And then, to top it all off, he did something unheard of—he drank from her Samaritan waterpot. Jewish religious custom held that to eat Samaritan food was equal to eating swine's flesh.

No wonder Jesus' disciples were flabbergasted when they saw him talking to her. Even these Galilean fishermen were not quite ready for this sort of indiscretion, but they knew Jesus well enough to keep their mouths shut and say nothing.

What a picture of the Savior! Here he is, heaven's holiest, doing everything his native religion forbade. But he had found in the Samaritan woman the kind of person he had come to help. And he did not let fear of criticism and misunderstanding stop him.

What feelings must have run through the soul of this poor, faded failure of a woman. At best she was a five-times divorcee and now a common-law wife. At worst she was a harlot.

Why didn't this Jew reject her as did everyone else? Why didn't this Rabbi draw up his holy garments and avoid her like every other rabbi? Why didn't he turn his back like the rest of the "good" people?

This Jew was strangely different from any other Jew she had ever met. He was different from any other man she had ever met. He was not afraid of her. He did not try to take advantage of her for a further cheapening of her soul. Instead, he talked to her about God and his love. He talked in strange terms about the water of life, about never coming to the well to draw water. Who was this Stranger by the well? How did he know so much about her?

Hope blazed in her bosom. Could this possibly be the Messiah? Yes, it was a possibility, for who else could be like him? She ran home shouting, "Come see a man who told me everything that I have ever done; this couldn't be the Christ, could it?"

She forgot her reputation. She forgot her waterpot. In her

excitement, she even forgot the stares and snubs. For a moment she forgot that she was a byword in Sychar. She had met Jesus, the friend of sinners. He had left her with the feeling that he believed she could be a better person. And because he believed it, she began to believe it, too.

I wonder how many other people are corrupt, hopeless souls just because nobody ever expected anything better of them? We are too ready to wag our heads and say, "Well, what else did you expect?" I wonder, too, how many would be dramatically different if they only had someone to believe in them.

Might not sinners of our day level this charge at us: "Christians have no dealings with Samaritans"? What would happen if a harlot walked into our Sunday worship services, or if our pastor were caught talking to one in the park? Would we cry; "Out, strumpet! Who wants the likes of you ruining the reputation of our church and pastor." Would the "pillars" in your church tremble with righteous indignation at such defilement of your lovely carpeted sanctuaries.

An ancient fable tells of a monarch who entertained all the beggars in the kingdom. The king gathered in the banquet hall all his courtiers, clothed in their lavish apparel. Beggars sat at the same table in their poverty and rags.

On such an occasion one of the courtiers had soiled his silk garments and could not remove the stain.

"What shall I do?" he thought. "I cannot go into the king's feast in this foul robe."

He sat weeping until a thought struck him. "Tomorrow," said he, "when the king holds his feast, some will come as courtiers decked in their beautiful array. Others will come and be made just as welcome in their rags. And if I cannot enter in my rich apparel, I will go in as a beggar."

On the morrow he sat among the beggars, but he saw the king just as well as if he had been arrayed in his scarlet and fine linen.

The Savior, likewise, welcomes all who come to him. If you cannot come as a saint, then come as a sinner.

One day, as Jesus sat quietly teaching the people in the Temple, a commotion suddenly started on the edge of the crowd. In came the scribes and Pharisees dragging a woman caught in the act of adultery (John 8:1-11).

These spiritual vigilantes preened themselves in their self-righteousness. They had no feeling for the woman, the crowd, or for Jesus. Right into the circle of faces they shoved her and cast their sordid accusation at her: "Master, this woman was taken in the very act of adultery." And I don't doubt that they said it with a good bit of relish.

With a sanctimonious air, they said, "Now Moses in the Law commanded us that such should be stoned, but what sayest thou?"

Shame and tension filled the air. The woman glared at her accusers. Her hate-filled eyes burned with contempt. The crowd dropped back, but they stayed to listen. Jesus was too embarrassed to speak.

He stooped down and traced something in the dust. It's anybody's guess what he wrote. I think he might have written the same Ten Commandments that the finger of God wrote on Sinai. Maybe he only doodled, giving himself and the woman time to regain their composure. Who knows? It's not important.

Jesus looked up and put the acid test to those pious hypocrites: He that is without sin among you, let him first cast a stone at her.

That did it. As he began to write again, her accusers began to sneak out. Like whipped curs, they tucked their tails and slipped away.

The word *sin* used here can mean sinful desires. Jesus could have been saying, "All right, stone her if you wish, but let the one of you who has never wanted to do just what she's done cast the first stone."

I've often wondered how those chaps managed to catch her in the act of adultery. They could have surprised her, but that is not likely. They probably knew more than they were willing to tell. At any rate, why didn't they drag in the man who shared her illicit romance? Why did they leave the poor woman to bear the disgrace and death penalty alone?

Count Tolstoy tells of stopping one evening at a tavern for a meal. A young girl with curly hair, red face, and swollen eyes sat at the counter.

"How do you make your living?" the Count asked.

"I hang around drinking saloons," she replied.

Not quite knowing what she meant, Tolstoy asked again, "What are your means of life?"

She laughed and gave no further answer.

At that moment the master of the lodging came in. He cast a stern look at her and said, "She's a prostitute, sir." Then he turned to the girl and with a surly air snapped, "You hang around the drinking saloons. Well! Give the answer you ought to give— prostitute."

Tolstoy said to the man, "You have no right to insult her. If men lived as God would have them live, there would be no prostitutes. We ought rather to pity them than to blame them."

When Jesus finally spoke to the adulteress, his words surprise us. "Woman, where are those thine accusers? hath no man condemned thee?" She replied, "No man, Lord."

Look at that answer from the adulteress. She called Jesus "Lord." The best the scribes and Pharisees could muster was "Rabbi." Small wonder Jesus said that harlots and publicans would enter the Kingdom and the Pharisees would be cast out. For Christ prefers a heart, no matter how soiled and in what shambles, that welcomes him to a heart that is perfectly clean and white, but cold and hostile.

The sullenness began to leave the woman's face. The hard lines softened. "Who is this man?" she asked herself. Never had she met anyone like him. Why hadn't he joined in her condemnation and approved her execution? Could it be that here was a man who thought of her as something other than dirt? Could this rabbi look upon her sins with something other than condemnation? Did he want to help her and not stone her?

Yes, it was true. And that remarkable man was Jesus—Jesus who still looks all guilty sinners in the face with grace and compassion.

How swiftly the Savior disposed of her doubts and fears. How sympathetically did he erase her shame and guilt. "Neither do I condemn thee: go, and sin no more."

This woman who had so shamelessly committed public adultery was still a person to Jesus. She was a soul to redeem, not a thing to be cast out. His revulsion at her sin was swallowed up in his pity. Jesus asked not, "What shall be done to her?" but, "What shall be done for her?"

She had broken the law of Leviticus 20:10. To the Pharisees, she deserved to die. But to Jesus, she deserved to be forgiven and restored. And that is just the difference between Jesus' attitude toward sinners and that of the Pharisees and scribes.

They were concerned with punishment. He was concerned with salvation. They were the merciless dispensers of judgment. He was the gentle dispenser of God's mercy.

How amazing that the holy Son of God would treat a sinner so graciously. But, then, that is just like him, isn't it? He had nothing to hide, no reputation to maintain. But he had a vision of what such moral lepers could be. And when sinners caught that vision, they, too, saw their possibilities. A word, a look, a kind act from the Savior and the most wayward were brought to repentance.

"Make yourself as black as you may," said a great old saint. "You cannot make yourself more than a sinner; and the gospel is for such as you are—for sinners."

On another day Jesus went to dine with an important Pharisee,

Simon by name. As they ate, a most remarkable thing happened. The town harlot interrupted the banquet.

What courage it must have taken for her to enter the "off limits" premises of a prominent Pharisee and weep over a rabbi. But the rabbi was Jesus, and she had reason to believe he would not rebuke her.

No doubt she had heard how he had befriended others like herself. Perhaps she had been hanging around the door, listening to his gracious words. We may never know what caused her to do what she did.

But this hard-bitten woman of the street whose reputation was common gossip in town slipped up behind Jesus. She began to pour her scalding tears over his feet. She broke the vial of perfume that she wore around her neck, and spilled its fragrance over the feet of the Master. The poor woman had no towel or napkin. Her long, dark tresses, the symbol of her trade, became the cloth with which she wiped the Savior's feet. She dared not kiss Jesus about the cheek. So she stooped and kissed his feet.

Poor self-righteous Simon could not understand these goings on—a sinner woman kneeling at the feet of Jesus crying her heart out and sacrificing the last cent she had in the world. Worse still, Jesus allowed the streetwalker to do it without so much as a rebuke. In fact, he seemed to enjoy it.

Simon thought he had such little need of repentance, and his cold heart was so slightly warmed by the Savior's presence. He had no capacity to understand the feelings of a forgiven sinner, for only a soul lost on the sea of sin can appreciate the depths of God's mercy.

Simon had not so much as treated Jesus to the common courtesies of a regular guest. He gave him no kiss of friendship. Neither did he put a drop of perfumed oil on the head of the Lord. He did not even give him water to bathe his feet.

I wonder why he even bothered to invite the Master. It was the thing to do, I suppose. After all, the young Nazarene was somebody. But once he had invited him he could, at least, have treated him with the courtesies of a casual guest.

The best Simon could muster was a muttering, "This man, if he were a prophet, would have known who and what manner of woman this is" (Luke 7:39). But he missed the point. Jesus did know, and because he knew he reached out to her.

Jesus rebuked Simon for his thoughtless hypocrisy. Then he turned to the woman and said, "Her sins, which are many, are forgiven" (Luke 7:47). She had sinned deeply; she loved deeply; and Jesus forgave freely.

An old Indian chief, hardened and calloused by years of war, had his heart transformed by the grace of God. He and an old cavalry officer were talking one day. "Tell me, Left Hand," asked the officer, "how are you such a changed man? How was it done?"

The Indian replied, "I cannot tell you, but I can show you."

They walked into the woods. The Indian raked together a pile of dry leaves, put a worm in the middle, and set the leaves on fire. When the worm felt the heat, it crawled to the other side. But there it met the fire. It rushed to the other side, and there was the fire. After several tries, the worm crawled to the center and up to die.

Just before the flames reached it, the Indian plucked the worm to safety. "There," he said, "that is the way God did it to me. I found myself a sinner. I felt in danger of the fire. I tried to save myself from the wrath to come. But wherever I went and whatever I did, I found fire. I ran to this side and to that, but met the fire. At last I gave up in despair. I saw how helpless I was. Then I looked up and said, 'Lord Jesus, save a poor sinner.' And Jesus took my soul right up."

Jesus felt what Simon could not feel and saw what Simon could not see. All Simon saw was a ruined reputation. Jesus saw a broken soul, begging for understanding and sympathy. The Savior

saw a poor, lonely creature, an object of God's redeeming mercy.
Simon saw a thing to be rejected. Jesus saw a soul in search of
forgiveness. Simon saw a town harlot who had shamelessly in-
vaded the privacy of his home. Simon saw through the eyes of
religion. Jesus saw through the eyes of God.

Jesus met another notable sinner in the city of Jericho—a fellow by the name of Zacchaeus.

The word spread throughout the city, "Jesus is here. Jesus is
here." The people heard it. Soon a large crowd of critics and
admirers gathered around the Savior.

Somewhere in the city a tax collector heard the news. He
wanted desperately to see the young rabbi he had heard so much
about. But how? He was short, and the crowd knew his face too
well. If they got a chance, they would even a lot of scores with
the one who had gouged them. If he tried to see over or get
through, he would get plenty of elbows in his ribs and kicks on
the shins.

What must he do? There was only one solution—climb the big
sycamore tree that hung over the road. Zacchaeus swallowed his
pride, forgot his position, and up the tree he went. (A rather un-
complimentary position for a government official, wouldn't you
say?)

The procession moved out of Jericho and along the road. Suddenly Jesus stopped. He was directly beneath the spreading limbs
of the large sycamore tree. The noisy crowd fell silent. Everybody
looked up. Perched on a limb sat Zacchaeus.

Jesus was arrested by a sight so rare. "Zacchaeus," he said,
"make haste and come down; for today I must abide at thy house"
(Luke 19:5).

What a surprise for the little publican. The best he had hoped
for was a passing look at the young Rabbi, or perhaps to hear a
word or two. But here he gets a personal invitation to come down.
And, what's more, Jesus invites himself to the tax collector's home.

In his wildest fancy Zacchaeus could never have dreamed of this.

He hit the ground with a bound and began giving his fortune to charity. He offered restitution for his wrongs beyond what the law required. The law required only the original goods plus one fifth. He offered to restore fourfold, as much as was required for a deliberate act of robbery or willful destruction of property. Zacchaeus seemed to be saying, "All right, if they think I'm so bad, I'll admit my sin as being of the worst sort; and I'll make amends."

The Jews of Jericho rated Zacchaeus as "the best hated man in town." To them, he was a cutthroat, traitor, stool pigeon, a louse. He was a sinner beyond redemption. But when Jesus saw the repentance in his soul, he cried, "He also is a son of Abraham" (Luke 19:9).

As the Lord of glory and the publican walked away together, the crowd threw this threadbare charge "that he was gone to be guest with a man that is a sinner" (v. 7). But Jesus knew, and still knows, where a welcome awaits him. So he passed up the homes of the "righteous" and went to dine with a sinner.

Christ saw beneath Zacchaeus' wealth and position. He saw the heart hunger that made a business executive shinny up a tree to catch a glimpse of the Carpenter from Nazareth. He saw the loneliness that drove him to seek the companionship of a fellow human who cared.

The gospel is "God in swineland" in search of sinners. It is God forsaking the ruts of religion and beating the bushes of the byways in search of vagrants and prodigals. God was in Christ, visiting the strange hostelries of the world, fooling around with the wrong people, going to the wrong places, and doing the wrong things to help sinners.

Jesus told the humorous story of the Pharisee and publican who went up to the Temple to pray (Luke 18:10-14). The Pharisee felt he was righteous and despised others, especially that publican back there. He looked down his pious nose at sinners. His prayer was an eulogy of himself, parading his virtures before God: "God, I thank thee, that I am not as other men are. . . . " He abstained from the common vices of men. But you will notice that his catalog of sins is rather short. He went beyond the Law by fasting twice a week and by giving tithes of all that he possessed. A real fine chap, wouldn't you say? Fine except for his hateful pride and his snobbish attitude toward publicans and other men.

The poor publican, struck with a deep sense of his sin, begged for the mercy of God. He knew he had no merit of his own and readily took his place as a sinner.

As the story closes, Jesus makes a startling announcement: "I tell you, this man went down to his house justified rather than the other" (Luke 18:14).

Did Jesus really mean that? Could a sinful tax collector be justified before God and a scrupulous Pharisee condemned? One kept the letter of the law and the traditions of the elders. The other ignored prescribed religious custom. One walked in the inner circles of Judaism. The other was an outcast.

Yes, Jesus said it; and he meant it. He knew that the man who knows he's a sinner and longs for forgiveness stands a far better chance of getting into the kingdom of God than the man who thinks he is as good as he needs to be.

A Quaker had visited his sick neighbor for many weeks. He talked to him about the needs of his soul. But the man always said, "I do not see what I have to be concerned about. I've never done anybody any harm in my life."

The Quaker noticed that the man slowly stopped mentioning his goodness. In time his heart grew tender.

One day the poor sick man burst out: "I am too great a sinner. There is no mercy for me."

"Thank God!" cried the Quaker. "I have hope of thee now."

Jesus told the lovely stories of the lost sheep, the lost coin, and the lost boy. The Savior is the Good Shepherd who leaves the ninety and nine in the pasture and goes in search of the one lost sheep. He is the woman who lights a candle, sweeps her house, and searches for the one lost coin. He is the gracious Father who falls upon the neck of the returning prodigal.

The Pharisees failed to get the point of these stories. They had no idea of a God who went in search of sinners and rejoiced when he had found one. The God of Jesus was the opposite. He came not to condemn the world, but that the world through him might be saved. He ransacked the universe, looking for sinners. He left his throne in search of lost souls. And he still watches and waits for returning prodigals. He welcomes them home even with the smell of the hog pen upon them.

Who but Jesus could ever have told us of a God so fair and generous. And how shall we describe his attitude toward sin but by this: tender mercy, faith, hope, kindness, and expectation toward the wayward and sinful; firmness toward sin; and harsh, uncompromising judgment toward hypocrisy.

Jesus came into the world to die for his enemies. He came to die at their merciless hands. They pursued his life from beginning to end, and at last they slew him and hanged him on a tree. Yet the Savior never returned a blow or a bitter word. As they pounded the nails through his flesh and bone, he prayed, "Father, forgive them; for they know not what they do" (Luke 23:34).

Shall we then recriminate and harbor resentment for real or fancied wrongs? Shall we carry about an unforgiving spirit and seek sweet revenge? When we are reviled, shall we revile again? Are we sullen with someone, refusing to go on in love? Has some petty grievance driven a wedge between you and your fellowman? Have you forgotten how much God for Christ's sake has forgiven you? Do you not remember the Scripture that says, "Let this mind be in you which was also in Christ Jesus" (Phil. 2:5)? Can you not, for Christ's sake, love and forgive your enemy or, for that matter, have no such person as an enemy?

It is so much easier to condemn than to grieve. A hasty, hard attitude goes easier with us than a broken heart. And we have a problem at the point of separating sin from the sinner. It is hard for us to have a holy hate for sin and a genuine love for the sinner. To do so requires the mind of Jesus, an ability to look beyond the scarred, stained surface to the lonely, lost soul beneath.

5

FISHERMEN AND TAX COLLECTORS

These were the men upon whom Jesus pinned the hopes of his kingdom. Simon and Andrew, James and John, Philip and Bartholomew, Matthew and Thomas, James the son of Alphaeus and Simon the Zealot, Judas the brother of James and Judas Iscariot—a motley crew of fishermen and tax gatherers, all Galileans, and one a traitor.

Did Jesus, the carpenter from Nazareth, really expect these men to go against the world? Ludicrous, isn't it? But that is the way it was, and that is the way he chose. History has proved our first impression and snap judgments of these twelve Galilean peasants wrong, for the world still wears the indelible imprint made by the sandals of these, the Master's men.

As Jesus sat to choose his band, a soft mountain breeze rippled the Sea of Galilee and fanned the people's flowing robes as a sea of brown faces stretched out before him. Mount Hermon shimmered like an emerald in the morning sun. The Jordan churned its way on toward the Dead Sea.

The Master had spent the night in prayer. Because, you see, this was the day he would choose the men who would carry on his work after his death. He needed more than ever his Father's wisdom. He could not afford any mistakes.

Ah, there they were, twelve men who had been with him for a few months now. They were sitting in front of the crowd, waiting and hoping he would choose them. Their eager, friendly faces looked so good in that sea of strangers and hecklers. Here were, at least, a few who believed in him; and he knew it would be they that he must choose.

He saw that look of revolutionary expectation on their faces. Because, really, what better way to begin a revolt than to choose a few loyal insurgents, train them, inspire their loyalty, and use them to organize an army of liberation? If revolution had been Jesus' goal, could he have made a better choice than this group of volatile leftist Galileans?

They were anxious to move on Rome. Peter patted his sword and swore his willingness to die at his Leader's side. Judas, Simon Zealotes, Thaddaeus, and James the son of Alphaeus quickly threw in with him. Even Matthew, the tax collector, was willing to come along. Jesus never quite got their revolutionary dreams out of them, for even after his resurrection they still wanted to know what he was going to do about restoring the kingdom to Israel.

He laid his standards out to these men. His standards were not the world's standards, and his kingdom was not of this world. In his kingdom, the smallest would be greatest, and the servant would be chief of all. The last would be first, for he had not come to be served. They could not expect to go in any grander style than their master.

They did not know, and could not know at the present, that it would only be a short while before Jesus would anger the religious establishment at Jerusalem. They would join hands with Rome to put him to death. But he did that day what he had to do. He chose these twelve men whom we call his disciples.

Many have often questioned and doubted his choice. They weren't much to look at, expecially at first glance. But they were what he needed, and he knew what they could become.

The world has often thought him daft, not simply because of the men he chose, but for the very idea that a Galilean carpenter would have the gall to set out to change the world with the help of such a wild assortment of men. But, you see, he had the advantage of us. He knew he was not alone in his choice. He knew that his mission was not an act of insanity. He knew that he came from his Father and that he would go back to him. He knew also that his Father would care for his work while he was in the world and care for the men he was putting in charge of it after he was gone. And do not be too quick to think he could have done better with men of a finer cut. You shall soon see that his choice was perfectly justified.

So much for men's opinion of the Master. It mattered little then, and it matters even less now. But let me tell you in a little more detail of these twelve that he chose to be with him.

They were ordinary men. But they were adventurers, not afraid to take a gamble, and not afraid to leave the security of their vocations to follow an unknown teacher. They were not great thinkers, and they were often bitterly prejudiced. They wore no halos and struck no pious poses to impress the public. These men did not bear a sweet expression of beatific smiles like they were etched in stained glass. They were men who loved the sea, adventure, and the outdoors. Best of all, they had huge capacities for discipleship. That mattered to Jesus. But what mattered most was that they were like him. With all their faults, and they were many, he would not have traded them for any other group of men on earth.

His men were not religious supermen, and they harbored no illusions about themselves. Peter knew he was a sinner; Thomas knew he was a natural-born pessimist. Matthew didn't try to cover up the fact that he was a collector of taxes for the Romans. Bartholemew was a skeptic; and they were all doubters, men who had to see before they believed. They were not "big shots"; and they were not afraid of a day's work, of pain, or even death.

They were like the world they were going to minister to. They were workers, radical nationalists, a scholar, a Roman stooge, and a terrorist. No, I'm afraid you would not have found these men listed in Jerusalem's "Who's Who in Religion in Israel." But they were passionate men, not cramped and squeezed by some absurd religious life-style. They were not worried about their public image, just a pack of regular fellows with adventure in their souls and nothing to lose by following the carpenter from Nazareth.

There were three sets of brothers: James and John, Andrew and Peter, Matthew and James, sons of Alphaeus. Two of these, James and John, were Jesus' own first cousins. (Their mother and his mother were sisters.) Judas Iscariot was a political terrorist. Simon Zelotes, Lebbaeus, and James the son of Alphaeus were Israeli guerrillas. Philip and Bartholomew were close personal friends. Thomas was a loner, wanting to be by himself when he had problems, Bartholomew was a scholar; Philip was an extrovert, always on the lookout for new friends. Matthew was a tax collector, a hireling who had bought his hated but lucrative business. A curious mixture. Add to these Peter and Andrew, James and John who were coarse men of the sea, tough and carefree.

Why didn't Jesus do better, you ask? And you object that little or nothing is written about half of these men. But I ask, who would have known the name of Caiaphas or Annas unless their names had appeared alongside that of Jesus and his men? And who would have known of Pilate, Herod, or any of the others without their names being in the gospels written by these Galileans? But, be that as it may, I will tell you why the Master chose them, why he made a decision that seemed to beggar the imagination and belie his sanity. They were men full of life, ready to follow him at the drop of a hat, men open to change and free from the straitjackets of organized religion. They were men of some vision, men willing to look at change as something other than a threat, men willing to make decisions, and open to the idea that God could love all men.

True, they were provincial villagers. Five of them were from the same town, two from another, and one from another. All were from within a day's travel of Nazareth.

They were filled with prejudice. Remember the day James and John wanted to call down the fire of God on the Samaritan village because the Samaritans refused them lodging. And another time they stopped a man from his ministry who was casting out demons in Jesus' name. And when Jesus was introduced to good old scholarly Nathanael, he cried out, "Can any good thing come out of Nazareth?"

They were often afraid and in the end ran away. Their faith was almost always weak, and they were so forgetful of the many miracles Jesus did. It seemed that they could never understand anything, especially that he would have to die. They fussed among themselves about matters of pride and prestige and complained that he had not been clear in his teachings. They were too hasty with people, stopping the children from coming to Jesus and blind beggars from asking for help. They grouched because he refused to set up a kingdom on earth, and joined in a plot to take him by force and make him King.

They refused to believe in his resurrection even after the women had seen him alive and told them. Thomas, you remember, made his stubborn boast, "I will not believe unless I feel the print of the nails in his hands and thrust my hand into his side. Even after Jesus had appeared to them, they decided to quit their work and go back to their fishing.

But they were willing men. When their Lord said go, they went. They were willing to leave their livelihood and follow him. And that mattered so much more than that they be famous men in the world.

Only a few of these men are remembered for any contribution

to Christ's work. One is remembered only for his doubts, and another because he was a traitor. Most of the rest are remembered only because their names appear in the lists of his disciples. But that should be of no great concern to us. He chose them and trusted them. Because he did, they went out and did what no other band of men in history has ever done.

And how much better off Jesus was with these men, with all their failings, than he would have been with a bunch of religious mollycoddles from Jerusalem that parted their hair in the middle and were forever adjusting their halos. He preferred these diamonds-in-the-rough to the well-polished doctors of the Law. At least these men had a cutting edge left. Life for them was never a dull gray. Religion was not a tame exercise in respectability. For these men, life was always full speed ahead, or all engines in reverse.

The Master preferred this band of disciples who were hard to control, but champing at the bits, to a group of suave, smooth promoters of the religious establishment, denuded of their humanity and zeal. He wanted men who were more concerned with people than with the fine points of theology, men who had their feet firmly planted on the earth and who spoke the language of the common man.

These men were full of their father, Jacob. There was a lot of human and a little angel about every one of them. Everything about them was not bad. When their Lord sent them to get a donkey from a man they had never seen, they had the faith to go with only the word that Jesus needed the animal. When he sent them to prepare the Passover, they went with only the word that they would see a man bearing a pitcher of water. When he sent them out on a missionary journey with nothing for food and shelter, they went, depending on his word and the goodwill of the people.

When the five thousand had to be fed, they could not imagine where Jesus would get the food. But it is to their credit that they

did what they could. They brought him the five loaves and two
fishes and had the people to sit down and prepare to be served.
At the last Passover, when he mentioned that one of them would
betray him, they all felt the sting of their failures and cried out,
"Lord, is it I?" They ran away when he was arrested and slept
while he prayed. They did not even come back to bury his body.
But they did come back, and when they came back, they went
everywhere preaching the Word. Peter, who had been so brave and
turned so cowardly, stood strong as the rock Jesus knew he would
become and preached the gospel.

Isn't it likely, then, that we ought to be a little slower in our
criticism of these men? I doubt that we would have done any
better. Most of us aren't doing any better now.

Jesus never made life easy for these men. He knew their work
would be like his work, and their fate would be like his fate. He
sent them out as lambs among wolves. He called them to forsake
family and friends, and he required them to take up their cross
daily and follow him.

The Master completely identified himself with his men. He that
received them, received him and his Father as well. He and his
Father would come to them and make themselves known to them
in a way that they would be known to no others. If they stood by
him and confessed him before men, he would stand by them and
confess them before the angels and his Father in heaven. He gave
them the presence of his Spirit and assured them that all the power
of heaven would be with them in their work.

Jesus knew they would be delivered up to councils, and
scourged in the synagogues. They would be arrested and tried
before kings and governors, imprisoned and put to death, betrayed by family, and persecuted from city to city. Not for one
moment did he tell them to expect anything different. Neither
for one moment did he ever leave them thinking he would desert
them.

The Carpenter had confidence in his men. He promised them that if they would follow him, he would make them fishers of men. He called them the salt of the earth, and the light of the world. He let them know that he had deliberately chosen them from among so many, and that he expected them to go and bear fruit in his service. He even told them that they would do greater works than he was doing and that they were to be his witnesses to all the ends of the earth.

Such confident boasting may sound to you like the rantings of a madman but they believed him. Because they believed him and knew that he believed in them, they went out into a wild, rampaging Roman Empire filled with the stink of moral decay and did things that still stagger the imagination of mortal men.

Now, let me tell you about each of these twelve men in more personal terms. Although they were all Galileans and may all seem so much alike, they were quite different. Each one was a distinct person in his own right, and you ought to know them as Jesus knew them.

Let's begin with John, shall we? We usually think of him as "the beloved"; but Jesus knew a different John, and knew him well. John was the younger brother of James. He was from a fairly well-to-do family. His father, Zebedee, owned a fishing business in Capernaum and had hired servants in his household. You remember, of course, that his mother, Salome, helped provide for Jesus and his disciples out of her own money.

John was a close personal friend to Peter and Andrew and had been a disciple of John the Baptist before coming with the Lord.

He was a hothead. Jesus didn't name him a "son of thunder" for nothing. He was as ambitious as he was hotheaded. (I suppose he got that from his mother.) He thought that he and his brother ought to be named the Lord's first assistants, one on his right hand and the other on his left, perhaps making a bit of political capital because of his importance and family ties.

Peter never forgot this absurd request. Even after Christ's resurrection, he asked, "And what about him?" Jesus reminded Peter that John's future was none of his business. His business was to follow him. But Peter was not by himself. The other disciples got into a fit of anger, and the Lord had to remind them that he was not in the business of handing out political favors. His Father would give the places of leadership in his kingdom to those who earned them. And besides, in his kingdom, the greatest of all must be servant of all. That cooled their ambitions a bit. But John still managed the best seat at the last Passover.

John's prejudice was about as strong as his ambition. He despised the Samaritans and had little love for the Judeans. He had no tolerance for those who were not numbered with the band of disciples, even if they were casting out demons in Jesus' name. They must stop. Jesus had to remind him that, if the man was not against him, he was for him.

Oh, no, I do not mean to paint John as a villain. But I do mean to show you that he was a man—an aggressive, impetuous, and sometimes belligerent Galilean. His zeal was often misdirected, and he was sometimes selfish. He, along with the other disciples, lacked insight into their Lord's mission.

But, in spite of John's failings, Jesus loved him. He was exciting to be around. The Master knew he possessed tremendous potential for good. So, he took him into the inner circle of his disciples and began to channel his zeal into service in his kingdom.

He was with Jesus at the raising of Jairus' daughter and on the mount of transfiguration. The Savior took him into the garden of Gethsemane the night he was arrested. He followed Jesus into the high priest's quarters when the Lord first went on trial.

His Lord entrusted him with the care of his mother at his crucifixion and he stood by Jesus' cross as he died. He was the first to know who the traitor was, the first to understand the significance of the empty tomb, and the first to recognize the risen

Lord that morning by the seaside.

The fire never really died out in John. In his later years, although he became a tender man and a deep thinker, he never had any tolerance for heresy and carelessness. He wrote fiercely against it in his epistles and his Gospel. It is said that John was in the bathhouse at Ephesus when Cerinthus, a noted heretic, walked in. John is reported to have fled the bathhouse clad only in a towel, crying, "Flee for your lives; Cerinthus, the enemy of all truth is in the bathhouse."

He became a pillar in the church and showed a courage that amazed the Jewish authorities. Even though he had been so prejudiced, he shared in the first mission to the Samaritans. Five books of our New Testament bear his name.

John was often imprisoned for his faith and strong preaching and was banished to the Isle of Patmos by the Emperor Domitian. He returned to Ephesus. There in his old age, when his memory was dim and he could only with great difficulty be carried to the church, he would say no more than, "Little children, love one another." When the church would ask him, "Why?" he would reply, "It is the Lord's command."

James, John's older brother, did not become as prominent among Jesus' disciples as his younger brother; but he was always a key man and a member of the inner circle. I think it is a testimony to his importance that when Herod Agrippa I reached out for a disciple to execute, he laid hands on James.

James, as you well know, shared his more prominent brother's traits. He, too, was a Salome in men's clothing—a robust "son of thunder" who was looking for the lion's share in Jesus' "revolutionary" kingdom.

It is not necessary for me to build James up. He was an excellent disciple in his own right, but he always had to walk in the shadow of his brother. His obituary in Acts, just two simple lines, is characteristic of this quiet, strong man who could be an effective disciple without being in the limelight.

Tradition says that James displayed such courage and faith at his death that the one who led him to the judgment seat was won to Christ. As they were led away to the executioner's block together, he begged James to forgive him. After a moment's reflection, James said, "Peace be with thee," and kissed him. The two were beheaded together.

Now to get to Peter—poor, lovable, miserable Simon Peter. Did you ever see such a mixture of strength and weakness, doubt and faith, fear and courage? On the one hand he boasted, I'll never desert you no matter what the others do." And then he was the first to run away. He was so brave in the garden when he was by the Savior's side, lashing out with his sword, quite willing to die. But out in the courtyard alone, a maiden scared him out of his wits; and he began to curse and deny that he knew the Man on trial inside. He went to sleep in the garden, and never showed up at the crucifixion. He forgot Jesus' warning but remembered the crowing of a rooster.

I remember so many humorous things about Peter. He so bravely stepped overboard to walk on the waters of Galilee but became wild with fright when he saw the churning waters about him. That day on the mount of transfiguration, Simon blurted out, "Let's build here three tabernacles," simply because he couldn't think of anything else to say.

He had given up quite a bit to follow Jesus, and he was quick to point that out to his Lord and to ask what he'd get in return. He felt that if he had forgiven his brother seven times, that was an abundance. He was flabbergasted that Jesus would suggest seventy times seven.

How shall I describe him? He was forward, leaping before he looked, a sharp contrast to his coolheaded brother, Andrew. He had a hasty tongue. His moods changed quickly and dramatically. He was rash and reckless, often shallow and wishy-washy. I'm sure the other disciples snickered when Jesus nicknamed him "The Rock." He was more like a willow bush.

Life for Peter was never dull. That fisherman was no pious religious corpse, mummified by tradition. He was high-tempered, impatient, and fretful. But he was a colorful, adventuresome man; rushing in where angels feared to tread. He was sometimes conceited, feeling himself just a cut above the others. His quick tongue often came to the rescue of the other disciples, and his recklessness frequently delivered them from the doldrums. He ran hot and cold; but when he was on fire, he transfused the others with his energy.

Peter was a true Galilean—passionate and sincere, frank and open, devoted and hardworking. He loved new ways of doing things, and was always ready for a change of pace. He, like all Galileans, was always spoiling for a fight with Rome. And that may be why he so readily joined up with the Nazarene.

Peter was just Peter, but Jesus loved him for being the person he was. He was always on hand for the big events in Jesus' ministry. Even at the last Passover, his curiosity got the best of him because he did not know who the traitor was. He always put in his bit and always wanted to know "Why?" He followed afar off, but it must be said to his credit that he followed. That is more than some of the Savior's men did. He was often in jail for his faith. He went about healing the sick and raising the dead. He dealt with church problems with the same vigor with which he fished and denied his Lord.

This fisherman from Bethsaida stood first among the disciples. He was the first to be a saint and first to be a satan. He recognized Jesus as the Messiah first and denied him most miserably. He was the first to leave his nets and the first to return to them. He preached the first sermon after Pentecost and created one of the first church problems. He was the first to support the gospel among the Samaritans and first to open the kingdom to the

Gentiles. He stood by Paul and the Gentile Christians at Jerusalem but yielded to Jewish pressure at Antioch.

Two books of our New Testament bear his name. Most agree that Mark is really Peter's gospel. Tradition says he was the first bishop of Antioch. He preached in Asis Minor, and he later went to Rome where he was crucified upside down because he was not worthy to die as his Lord.

Andrew, like James, lived in the shadow of his outspoken brother. If Andrew had wanted to be prominent, Peter would not have let him. But Andrew was a valuable disciple in his own right. He, along with James and John, was a disciple of John the Baptist. He was a sensitive, spiritually alert man, looking for and expecting the coming of the Messiah. Because of this, he was one of the first two disciples to meet Jesus. Then he went immediately to get Peter. That is what you will find Andrew doing—bringing others to Jesus.

Andrew was always known as "the brother of 'you-know-who,' " and that is not an easy situation to live with. But he was just that big. He could ride in the back seat and never complain. He was modest, unassuming, and steady; never in the inner circle and never the chief of anything. But he was a deeply loyal man, content to just be faithful and fill his place. He cared little for credit, but was always on hand when needed. Without Andrew, Peter would never have made it.

He was an optimistic man and a man of action. When the great crowds were hungry and Jesus had no food, it was Andrew who brought the boy with the bread and fish to the Savior.

Andrew was always interested in others. He was a man of decision, and the first of all the disciples to bring Gentiles to the Savior. Tradition has it that Andrew went as a missionary to the Scythians, a particularly crude, barbaric people, and that he died a martyr in Greece, tied to his cross to prolong his misery by starvation and exposure.

Like Andrew, Philip had a missionary heart. He was the first to whom Jesus said, "Follow me." As soon as he met the Master, he went for his friend, Nathanael.

Philip's home was also Bethsaida, the hometown of Peter and Andrew, James and John. He, like his fishermen friends, was a practical man. Remember the day when Jesus needed to feed the multitudes? He asked Philip how much it would take. He had already figured the problem out and had decided that there was no way. Why, two hundred denarii wouldn't buy enough for everybody to have a crumb. Besides there were no markets in the wilderness.

So, Jesus asked him what he did have. With a shrug of his shoulders and a what's-the-use look, he replied, "Only five pitifully small barley loaves and a couple of pickled fish." Then he shot a look at the Savior that said, "But what good will that do?" Good old practical Philip had forgotten what Jesus could do. His good business sense got in his way.

Philip was no headliner, but he was an intelligent man with a quick grasp of things. When the Greeks came to see Jesus at the Passover, he knew the Lord's association with Gentiles could spell more trouble. So, he talked the matter over with Andrew before bringing them to the Savior.

And at the last Passover, Philip still wanted everything spelled out. He coolly told Jesus, "Show us the Father, and it will be enough proof." Let's not be too critical of Philip's practical blindness for he had asked the question the others wanted to ask. Time was running out. Philip seemed to sense it. When Jesus gently rebuked him for his lack of insight, he was rebuking the others as well.

Papias refers to Philip as one of the elders. It is likely that he died and was buried at Hierapolis.

Who should I mention next but Philip's best friend, Bartholomew, whose first name was Nathanael. It is no small wonder these two were bosom pals. They were just alike—skeptical, if not a bit cynical. When Philip mentioned that Jesus was from Nazareth, Nathanael's jaw fell open, and he cried out, "Can anything good come out of that hillybilly, hick town, Nazareth?"

Philip did the right thing. He knew his friend, and simply replied, "Come and see for yourself." Men like Nathanael are never satisfied with arguments. They always demand proof. Jesus knew his stripe and challenged him on his own ground. "Nathanael," he said, "before Philip called you, I saw you under the fig tree." Ah, that took him up short; and in typical Galilean style, he jumped to the conclusion that Jesus was in fact the Messiah.

Do you wonder why Jesus called Bartholomew to be a disciple? Why didn't he just let him alone in his bigotry? Because he needed men like him, that is why. He was not only a skeptic. He was a deep man of prayer and a scholar. And when this kind of man is convinced, he makes the best of disciples.

Jesus simply stripped away Bartholomew's doubts and airs of superiority. "Well, well, what have we here? An Israelite in whom there is no guile?" Nathanael got the point quickly. But Jesus prodded him a bit more. "Are you so quickly convinced? You shall see greater things than these. Yes, you'll see even greater things than Jacob experienced at Bethel."

You see, Jesus knew that Nathanael was a good student of the Scriptures. He knew the man would be a valuable disciple if he could win him, for the Master's men would have to bear witness to scholars as well as ordinary men.

Bartholomew is said to have been of royal ancestry. If so, he made an interesting addition to this band of fishermen and tax gatherers who followed the Galilean. Tradition describes him as having curly black hair, white skin, large eyes, a straight nose, and long, grizzled beard. He was of medium height and wore a royal robe with a gem at each corner, and he was an expert in the Law and prophets.

Matthew was one of Jesus' favorite disciples. He belonged to that outcast group called publicans—Roman lackeys who collected the hated tribute money. I am sure you think it very strange to find a Roman collaborator in Jesus' band; but you shouldn't be so surprised, for the Master had received his warmest welcome from these "sinners."

I almost laughed when I learned of a publican with the patriotic name of Levi. I suppose his parents must have been terribly disappointed to have a son named Levi turn out to be a flunky of the Herods. To make bad matters worse, his brother, James the son of Alphaeus, was an Israeli guerrilla.

I suppose you think it even stranger still that the Messiah would enlist a Roman agent for a disciple. It does, I am sure, defy all that is called good judgment. But Jesus often defied deep-rooted tradition and flew in the face of popular opinion. Nobody, and I do mean nobody, was more bitterly hated by Jesus' people than were the Roman revenue agents. They were regarded as quislings who bought their jobs and sold their souls in the deal. They operated on a percentage of the take. The more they took, the richer they got; and many of them got wealthy through graft and extortion.

Jesus' choice of Matthew, if he hoped to be accepted as the Messiah, seems to border on insanity. One hardly expects to be acclaimed for his patriotism when he befriends a fifth columnist. Jesus needed Matthew, and Matthew needed Jesus. That is reason enough for the Master's choice.

Matthew's collection office was by the Sea of Galilee near Capernaum. And, no doubt, he had heard Jesus preach many times. He had heard him tell of God's love for all men, and his desire to forgive sinners. His heart ached. For he was considered vulgar by Rome and despised by his own people. He was classed with murderers and robbers and was barred from worship and responsible civic duties. Friendless, lonely, and hating his business, he felt he was beyond all hope until Jesus came.

When he met the Nazarene, hope came alive again. His message of God's love and acceptance went straight to his heart. He quickly left his lucrative trade to join up with a band of men who had nothing. Who doesn't need a man like that?

Jesus had another reason for calling Matthew. He knew that the world teemed with publicans who wondered if God's love was for them—people at the bottom of the barrel, unloved and forgotten. Could he make a difference to them? He could and he did. Levi called a great number of his cronies together for a banquet in honor of his Friend from Nazareth. The Savior won so many of them that he soon became known as the "friend of publicans and sinners." And amazingly enough the Gospel that is most detailed and most thoroughly Jewish bears the name of Matthew.

Matthew's brother, James the son of Alphaeus, is not a prominent name among Jesus' disciples. In fact, he is nicknamed "The Less," probably because of his size; but it is a fitting description of his position. He always stands in the shadow of James, the brother of John. Matthew eclipsed him as well. But do not think him unimportant, because for every Peter and John there must be a million men who are willing to do their job and be called "The Less." And these "Lesses" are as loved by Jesus as their more prominent brothers.

Another of Jesus' disciples that was an unknown but courageous man was Thaddaeus. His real name was Judas son of James; but somehow he had earned two nicknames, Thaddaeus (the bold one) and Lebbaeus (the hearty one). I think he most likely earned these names as a lusty, courageous enemy of Rome.

To be sure, Thaddaeus was no coward. And perhaps he often filled the disciples' evening with fun and tales of his guerilla exploits. Jesus liked Lebbaeus because he lived life with zest. He stood up to criticism and threw himself into his work with robust enthusiasm. He loved the challenge, the excitement, and the action of his calling.

Jesus must have laughed the day he blurted out, "Let's get on with it. Show yourself to the world now." He wanted his Lord to become a popular hero, and the quickest way was too slow for him. Jesus' heart must have gone out to him at the last Passover when he cried out, "Why all this talk about dying?" Thaddaeus was that kind of man, just the kind our Lord's kingdom needed.

Do you think it strange that the teacher of love would call into his band a man like Simon the Zealot? It is true that he was a member of the Israeli underground, a man fanatically devoted to the violent overthrow of Rome and the liberation of Israel. He was a hard man with no fear of death and felt no twinge at killing.

He was completely devoted to a "holy war" against Rome, a political descendant of the great Maccabees. He loved adventure and hated the establishment. Many of his friends lost their lives when Masada, their last stronghold, fell to the Romans in A. D. 73. With all hope of escape gone, their commander, Eleazar, urged them to kill their wives and children and then commit suicide. They immediately embraced their wives, kissed their children, and set about the bloody work.

Why did Jesus choose Simon? Jesus needed him. He was strong, not afraid of death or torture, fearless in the face of opposition. He shunned the usual modes of society, longed for change, and needed a cause to live and to die for.

Jesus chose him because he wanted to cleanse him of his hatreds and use his courage for his kingdom. He wanted to reach out to other Zealots and to see if a tax collector and a guerrilla could be brought together in his love. He did not fail, for they were still together after his resurrection. The cross had won over the sword, and his hatred for Rome turned to love for Christ's kingdom.

A lovely tradition tells us that he and Jude went to Russia where they chose martyrdom rather than the death of their captors.

Thomas is best known to us for his doubts, but he was no greater doubter than any of the rest of the disciples. He was simply more open and vocal about it. Let it be said to his credit, that when the evidence was in, he believed just as strongly as he had doubted. His confession was even more sure than Peter's. For Thomas, it was not a "Thou art" confession, but it was a "My Lord, and my God." Much more personal, wouldn't you say?

Thomas was more of a plodder than a doubter, the typical workhorse of any crowd. One outburst branded him forever as a "doubting Tom." He was a man of real courage even if a bit pessimistic. Often he saw nothing ahead but darkness, but he was not afraid of it. When Jesus prepared to return to Judea for the last time, Thomas expected him to be killed. He was quite ready to go die there with his Lord. He did not let his doubts interfere with his loyalty.

Thomas was never ashamed to admit his doubts and ask his questions. He simply spilled out what was on his mind, and usually what was on everybody else's mind as well. When he said in the upper room, "Lord, we do not know where you are going, and how can we know the way?" he was simply putting into words the thoughts of the other disciples.

Thomas was never of the stripe that is always full of stupid questions that never seek an answer, but only to debate. He merely wanted to be sure, and who can fault him for that? It is to the everlasting credit of Thomas that he made the critical discovery of the Christ for himself.

We come at last to Judas Iscariot, that supreme enigma of all time. You shudder at the mention of his name. I do not find it pleasant to talk about him either. And it is with deep sorrow that I remember. I particularly regret that the most honored name in Israel, Judah, was brought to lowest infamy by Iscariot's black deed.

Judas was not the man from Kerioth as many have supposed.

He was a *sikarios*, a professional killer, sworn to murder and destroy the hated Romans. And he was the son of a *sikarios*. His life from childhood had been filled with stories of violence, killings, and hatred. Dark plots, midnight forays against Roman garrisons, and assassinations had filled him with a callous disregard for human life.

He, no doubt, joined Jesus' band, hoping he would swiftly lead an attack on Rome. When his plan was frustrated, whatever loyalty he had turned to spite. Spite turned to hate. He sought revenge by betraying the Nazarene to his enemies.

Did Jesus know from the beginning that Judas was the kind of person he was? Of course, he knew all along that he was a dangerous man with a twisted mind; but he loved him in spite of it. He desperately wanted to help him and all others like him. For, you see, Judas had great potential for good as well as for evil. Had the Master been able to redeem him, what an asset he would have been to his kingdom. All those violent energies of his could have been salvaged, and he would have been a grand example to others like him.

It seemed that Judas had lost all desire to be better or different. Murder and thievery had become a way of life with him. He had gone too far into darkness. He came to hate everything and everybody and to think only of his cause. His life of stealth and murder had driven him into the hands of Satan, and Christ was never able to rescue him. He never gave up trying until the final bargain was struck, and he turned his back on Jesus forever.

Judas was so close to Jesus, and yet so far away. I'm sure the Savior often looked into his troubled eyes and at the hard lines in his face, and wished he could help. He even chose him to be one of his band, and he bestowed many favors on him. He appealed to him at every opportunity, but Judas' mind and heart were captive of a strange irrestistable brooding. He never saw the good in anything, and even complained of Mary wasting the precious ointment she poured over Jesus.

Satan drew the mantle of darkness over Judas' mind, and he eventually lost all feeling for right. Life became totally black, filled with bitterness and distrust. At last he betrayed not only Jesus' trust but that of the other disciples as well. And only Satan could have inspired him to do it in such a fiendish way. He chose the secret place of prayer in the garden as the place for his infamous deed, and the kiss of friendship was the signal to Jesus' captors. He led the mob there for a few pieces of silver, and he sold not only his Savior but his own soul as well. I can hardly imagine how the soul of the Savior must have recoiled within him as those traitorous lips pressed against his holy cheek.

Did Jesus ever forgive Judas? Judas never asked his forgiveness; he never wanted it. He never realized until too late what he had done. He did not, by this time, really believe that Jesus was the Messiah. What was one more dead man, more or less, to a man who had killed so often?

But the light of day came, and the truth dawned on him. He could not stand to live with his deed. The choice he had made could not be revoked, and he was awash with his own guilt. There was only one thing to do. Give the money back and destroy the thing that had done this black deed. Satan was finsished with him and cast him aside. And Judas died a suicide, not because of his love for the Savior but because of his hatred for himself.

You ask, "Could Judas have been different?" That is not the right question. Of course, he could have, at some point in life. But, you see, he leaped over the cliff into permanent spiritual darkness. The Savior had to watch him go as eternal darkness closed about him.

It was not that Judas couldn't be different. He wouldn't be different. He was what he was because he chose it that way. He could never bring himself to acknowledge Jesus as his Lord, even though he was numbered with his disciples. Rabbi was the

best he could ever muster. Although Jesus got him to live in his
company, he could never get him to share in his Spirit. The darkness was too deep.

These were the twelve who walked with the Savior. All but one
remained faithful and took up his work after his death. They were
a strange assortment of men, and it strikes me that Jesus must have
been a singularly strong person to have appealed to them.

They were all changed men, all but Judas. They lived with Jesus,
watched him, listened to him. Slowly they became more and more
like him. They were a simple band of Galilean peasants who, as
they beheld his glory, were changed into the same image.

Like Mencius, the ablest expounder of the Confucian system,
their chief wish was to learn to be like their Teacher. Our world
still echoes with their soft tread and feels the rays of their light.

6

THE ESTABLISHMENT

From his first lusty cry in the cow stall in Bethlehem until he climbed Calvary, the Nazarene was in perpetual conflict with the religious establishment. His first public act, the cleansing of the Temple, set him on a collision course with Pharisaism. His mission, to bring men to a living faith in God, clashed immediately with an arthritic religious system whose spiritual joints had calcified with rigid legalism. The end result of that clash was the execution of the young Rabbi from Galilee.

Religion was flourishing in Jesus' day. Converts were being gathered in. Temple coffers were overflowing—even at the expense of making the Gentile Court a stockyard and lining the house of God with tellers' cages. Hardsell methods were being used by slick salesmen of religion to enrich Judaism and extend its influence.

Underneath this thin veneer of religiosity a deadly disease was at work. Pharisaism had arisen to preserve the faith of Israel. The scribes arose to study, copy, and teach the Scriptures. A noble purpose, wouldn't you say? But the arteries of institutionalism had hardened. Doctrine was divorced from the Spirit of God. Hard, literal legalism had supplanted the spirit of the law. The voice of the prophet had fallen silent, and the religious manager had taken control. A once proud, spiritual representative of God had sunk to the depths of a petrified mummy of religion. A warped, blind conservatism led Judaism to crucify the Son of God.

Pharisaism had become a well-defended castle of religious pride and prejudice, a bastile of legalism, erected to protect what was accepted and approved in religion. Its faith had become so intertwined with the national ambitions of Israel that any real call to repentance was impossible. Religion had become the handmaid as well as the protector of established customs. To be against the system was religious as well as political suicide.

Yet Jesus never dodged the inevitable consequences of his clash with the establishment. He threatened their ecclesiastical power structures and thrashed them for substituting human tradition for the laws of God. But it was like attacking Jericho with a slingshot. The stones of institutionalized religion effectively resisted every effort of the Savior to let in the light of God. Jesus failed to crack the walls of first-century Judaism, but it is to his credit that he never stopped trying.

Jesus was not sour on Judaism. After all, it was his ancestral faith. His clash with the Pharisees was not by choice. He came to save, not to condemn; but he could not stand aloof while the faith of Israel drowned in the septic tank of professional religiosity. He attacked, not the true faith of Israel, but a Pharisaism that produced a spiritual paralysis by reducing dynamic spiritual experience to dogma and theological equations. And that brittle system of rules and requirements stifled the life experience of personal faith in God. It converted a faith that was to be a savor of life unto life into a stifling religion that became a savor of death unto death.

God does not operate according to theological schemes and stagnant patterns. He moves according to life needs and living experiences. God is not dead doctrine, but dynamic activity, ever changing, growing, flexing, and refusing to be capsuled into a doctrinal statement. That, more than anything else, was the root of the conflict between Jesus and first-century Judaism. New wine must forever burst old wineskins that will not yield to its living, moving force.

Jesus quickly learned as do all preachers who dare to speak their own conscience, that it is impossible to be a prophet of God while on the payroll of the people. For nothing strikes with a swifter vengeance, when threatened, than a religious system that has become the guardian of accepted social customs and political aspirations.

In that sort of religion, form replaces faith, living experience dies, the establishment takes over, and the true Word of God becomes captive to what is generally accepted and approved by the system. The cocoon is mistaken for the living creature that has long since flown. The mummy of ritual is painted, pampered, protected, and garnished to keep up the appearance of life.

Let the church in the twentieth century beware lest it become an enclave of religious isolationism, for Pharisaism was not always a reactionary religious establishment. In fact, it began as a progressive force for revival. The Pharisee' ancestors were political liberals, supporting John Hyrcanus as well as the Maccabean revolt.

They could count among their forerunners no lesser light than Ezra. Their ambition had been to assure Israel that she would never again go into captivity because of disobeying the Law. Therefore, their first step was to establish the content of the Law. Their second step was to "make a hedge" about the Law so there would be no possibility of breaking it either through intent, ignorance, or accident.

But their hedge became a wall of reaction that rose higher and higher until it shut out everything that threatened truth as it saw it. Pharisaism could brook no rival to its interpretations, no threat to its vested interests. So, this movement of God was soon owned by the priests, and Christ was sent to the cross.

The Pharisees' neurotic concern was with the picky points of their tradition. They had become fence tenders, not men on mission. Rather than continuing in their great tradition as lay revivalists and leaders of a populist revolt, the Pharisees degenerated into a power-conscious status group whose clout lay in the fact that they were the dispensers of the faith.

The latter became more important than faith. Right ritual became more important than obedience to God. Self-preservation took center stage, and their mission faded into forgetfulness. They taught a law that had no real influence in their lives, and their profession was that of extending their religious system rather than bringing men face to face with God.

Jesus saw through this skim of religion to the seething hypocrisy underneath. He recognized wineskins that would not tolerate his revival of the issue of personal faith in God. He saw a system that "nitpicked" his teachings, calling him sabbath-breaker, when his only crime was to heal a sick man.

Poor blind souls! How blind could they be? Blind enough to shut their eyes to the Son of God and flee away into the tombs of their beloved establishment, blind enough to destroy their Messiah who was bold enough to tell them the truth.

This obnoxious blindness generated a faithlessness that was forever badgering Jesus to show them a sign. It created a fanatical devotion to human tradition rather than the Word of God. It made religion a center of vested interest, and a burden to those conscientious enough to try to live by its regulations.

The Pharisees were forever needling Jesus about some picky point of the Law. They whined, "He can't be the Son of God. He does not keep the sabbath." Jesus politely reminded them that his Father worked; therefore, he worked. At that "blasphemy" they flew into a fit of religious rage.

But the Savior brushed aside their complaints about his neglect of religious ceremony. He condemned their meticulous observance of ritual to the neglect of spiritual principles. They carefully tithed the kitchen spices, but neglected the greater matters of justice and mercy.

The Pharisees strained their milk lest they swallow a drowned gnat, and thereby violate their law against eating strangled beasts. But they swallowed the camels (equally unclean animals) of prejudice and hypocrisy. They wore long faces when they fasted and prayed loud prayers in public. They carefully washed the outside of their cups, and whitewashed their tombs lest they stumble over one and be defiled. But they ignored the inner man and true righteousness.

Jesus had little time for the ceremonial side of their religion. Sabbath observances, many washings, and abundant sacrifices mattered little to him. Ritual and tradition were trifling matters. A right life before God was far more important than a right order of worship. God and his love reaching out to man in his need were the things that mattered to the Master. Sin was disobedience of God, not failure to follow proper ceremony. Defilement of the man came from the heart, not from stumbling over a grave or failing to wash properly.

Bawling cows and bleating sheep brought no satisfaction to God. Altars spattered with blood, the smoke of incense, and the stench of burning flesh could not replace repentance and faith. Great festivals and solemn assemblies divorced from obedience were an abomination.

In his never-ending battle with the deadening forces of ritualism, Jesus did not walk alone. The prophetic spirit was reborn in him as he joined hands with the other great prophets of God. He added his voice to their voices, crying in the wilderness of religious hypocrisy.

The Savior's favorite passage was Hosea 6:6, "For I desired mercy, and not sacrifice; and the knowledge of God more than burnt offerings." He joined Joel as he pled, "Rend your hearts, and not your garments." Amos, that fiery shepherd-prophet from the hills of Tekoa, reminded an ingrown religion that God despised their feast days and solemn assemblies. Isaiah told Israel that without obedient hearts the multitude of their sacrifices were useless. Samuel said that the Lord had far greater delight in obedience than in great sacrifice and a multitude of burnt offerings. Micah joined the spirit of Jesus in reminding Israel that God was more pleased with justice and mercy than with ten thousands of sacrifices and rivers of oil.

Jesus finally declared war on the guardians of customary religion. He battled a Judaism that had become an echo of popular opinion rather than the voice of God. It was a defender of the religious *status quo* rather than the faith once delivered. It was more concerned with propagation of itself than propagation of the Kingdom of God. Its purpose was maintenance, reproduction, and preservation. Judaism sought to save its life, and in the process lost it.

Are we any better today? Not at all. We are more concerned with the skills of merchandising our religion than with preaching the gospel. The church is rapidly approaching first-century Pharisaism. It is becoming more and more a palace guard, and less and less a band of spiritual commandos. We have more wordly cunning than we do the cutting voice of judgment.

True, we do not offer the blood of bulls and goats in our sanctuaries. But we do have our little Sunday ritual. And having faithfully recited it, we go on our way feeling very good about the whole affair.

Surely God must be pleased with us. We have dutifully visited our temples, said our prayers, and offered our sacrifices. Surely it cannot matter that we so quickly forget and begin to smite with the fist, curse, covet, lie, cheat, and destroy.

We spend our time promoting the institution and weaving the tapestries of the denomination. Most of our preaching is against little sins—shorts, lipstick, and the dance. But we neglect the weightier matters of justice and brotherhood. How often are oppression, prejudice, and greed touched by the church? They are the "no-noes" of a pulpit occupied by a proclaimer of folk religion approved by the people.

But that sort of religion is enemy number one of true Christianity. It is a spiritual deformity that comes from a slight exposure to the real thing. It is a reasonable substitute. Having gotten it, men are forever thereafter innoculated against genuine salvation. The spirit of self-righteousness blinds them to their true spiritual needs. It is a narcotic of the soul, a false satisfaction that promises what it can never give.

I have an uncomfortable feeling that if Jesus were here today he would first cleanse the church. With a whip of cords, he would lash out at the forces that have converted the ship of life into a museum for the display of ornamental religion. In bitterness, he would drive out an odious religious attitude that smells of Pharisaism and has little interest in anything but self-propagation. Then, I think Jesus would take to the sidewalks, parks, and taverns to gain a hearing for his gospel, for Jesus would have no more patience with our spiritual blindness than he had with that of the Pharisees.

The Italian sculptor, Antonio Canova, was about to begin his statue of Napoleon. They brought him a splendid block of marble at great expense. But his keen eye detected a tiny red line running through the upper portion of the block, and he refused to lay a chisel on it.

When the great John Hancock Building was under construction in Chicago, every precaution was taken. Construction men dug deep and poured the huge pilings on bedrock. Tons and tons of concrete were poured into its supports They were slowly and carefully cured.

To the eye, they were perfect. But the engineers took no chances. They X-rayed to see if there were any flaws. Deep within the concrete pilings they found gaping cavities caused by trapped air.

Jesus did not fall for the tricks of the scribes or walk into their traps. He saw through them, met their cunning at every turn, and handily defeated their shrewd schemes. They had tangled with no fool when they took on Jesus. He was a champion, as keen as a Saracen sword.

He blistered them with the Sermon on the Mount. His little stories of the widow's mite and the rich man and Lazarus were stinging rebukes to a power conscious, wealthy, religious system. His parables of the fruitless fig tree and the wicked husbandmen cut them to the quick. When the occasion demanded it, he was not above denouncing their hypocrisy with bitter woes of condemnation.

So blind were the Pharisees that they looked on the works of God and said, "He's casting out demons by the power of Beelzebub, the prince of demons." They went up in a huff at the claims of Jesus and shouted, "Say we not well that you are a Samaritan and have a devil" (see John 8:48). Like whimpering children playing in the street, they said of John, "He has a devil," and of Jesus, "He is a winebibber and a glutton."

These doctors of the Law could see well the crimes of the publicans and harlots. They could descend in pitiless judgment upon the poor who had neither time nor money to study and keep the tradition of the elders. But they were too blind to see the envy, greed, hate, jealousy, and arrogance in their own hearts.

In the caves of Kentucky there are millions of tiny crustacea. They are soft and white and blind. These tiny creatures were carefully examined by a biologist. He discovered that they had eyes, but the optic nerves were shriveled. Lack of use had rendered their eyes totally useless. They had not seen for so long they could not see.

When the Bastille was about to be destroyed, a prisoner was brought out who had lain for years in a dungeon cell. Instead of rejoicing at the light of day, he begged to be carried back into the gloom. He had been so long in darkness that the light of the sun only pained him. His comfort was to die in the dark prison that for so long had been his home.

To be spiritually blind and yet to be unconscious of our blindness is a monstrous calamity. To be blind and yet think we can see is to fall into a pitiable state where our illusions take on the air of reality. It is a drastic state where a man finds no forgiveness. For in his self-righteous conceit he seeks none.

It would be far better for any man to never have seen the light of the gospel than to, having seen it, shut his eyes to its light. Better would he be to be blind altogether than to see the truth and obey it not. To see Jesus and yet fail to recognize him as God's Son is to call down upon ourselves a far greater condemnation.

There is no blindness like a blindness that refuses to see. It looks at light and calls it darkness. Black is white, and white is black. The crooked is straight, and the straight is crooked. It sees nothing divine in Christ, is conscious of no sin, and cannot recognize goodness. It inverts moral values and calls good evil.

Few people ever degenerate to the point of Milton's Satan who said, "Evil, be thou my good." But the danger is always there for all men. Every stubborn rejection of the truth draws the mantle of spiritual darkness a little lower until, at last, lost in the night of spiritual blindness, we take a final leap into the dark.

Pharisaism condemned Jesus as well as all who would not condemn him. Nicodemus, a Pharisee, was threatened because he dared speak up for simple justice in Jesus' case. The man born blind was thrown out of the synagogue because he would not lie about the One who healed him. Furious over the popular acclaim due the Savior at the triumphal entry, they plotted to kill Lazarus who was a living testimony of the Galilean's power. Even those sent to arrest Jesus were accused of being deceived when they commented on Jesus' wisdom. If justice be blind, Pharisaism was a prime example of pristine purity. For its optic nerves were shriveled, and it shut its eyes to every evidence of Jesus' deity. In their stubborn prejudice the Pharisees determined to kill him. He was too dangerous to let live. He must die for he was too great a threat to their position and system.

The Pharisees were not above forming a bizarre alliance with the Sadducees, the Herodians, and the hated Romans in order to get Jesus. They screamed, "Crucify, crucify, crucify," when Pilate sought to release the Savior. When Pilate asked, "Why?" their bitter retort was "We have a law, and by that law he ought to die." They even went to the limit of bringing power politics into play, and of swearing allegiance to Caesar. Do anything. Just get that troublemaker from Nazareth.

They lied, bribed, and murdered; but they would not enter the Roman court lest they be defiled. Ha! Such hypocritical stupidity. They were perfectly willing to pay Judas to betray Jesus, but they could not accept again the "blood money." They bent every nerve and muscle to bring Jesus to the cross. But they just couldn't leave this body on the cross on the sabbath. Now that would be an awful sin, wouldn't it? How perverted can a religion and a people be?

It is difficult to believe that a religion that supposedly represented God could ever become so twisted as to murder his Son. Think of the blood-letting that has gone on in the name of God. There have been "holy wars," witchcraft trials, and execution of heretics aplenty. All in the name of God. Such a religion has always been, and is now, a millstone about the neck of God.

Someone has said that "the most converted are the most perverted." And the only people who outdid the Pharisees in their fanatical devotion to their religion were their Gentile proselytes. No wonder Jesus condemned the Pharisee for compassing land and sea to make a convert, and when he is made he is more of a child of hell than before. No greater error is ever made than to win a man to a church or religion and not to Christ.

There is no pervision like religious perversion, no meanness like that sanctified by the name of God. Today, this rank pharisaical sectarianism blocks the door to the kingdom of God to all but those who comply with its narrow and prejudiced views. It professes a monopoly on God's plan of salvation and consigns to hell all who do not submit to its petty interpretations.

Nineveh repented at the preaching of Jonah. That wicked Assyrian city recognized him as a true prophet. But a greater Jonah had come to Israel, and they crucified him. The Queen of the South traveled many miles to hear Solomon, but a greater than Solomon had come. Israel would not so much as cross the street to hear him.

The Jews thought Sodom to be unqualifiedly wicked and well deserving of their fate. Nineveh was so perverse that God threatened total destruction within forty days. What about a Judaism that confronted God in Christ, shut its eyes to the light and said, "We will not see"? Its damnation will be far greater because it has rejected the greater light.

What about men today who do the same? Will God be any less stern with them? He will not. They have had more light than even the Jews of Jesus' day. Do you think that God will not take this into account at the judgment?

Jesus could not compromise with scribal legalism and blind Pharisaism. So it judged him and set out to destroy him. In judging Jesus, Judaism judged itself. Its blind rejection left the Savior no choice but to pronounce God's judgment upon it. Pharisaism crucified Christ, but before he died, he signed that religious system's death certificate.

Jesus took no delight in his judgment of the Jews. Nay, rather, his heart was crushed within him. As he made his final journey to Jerusalem he broke into uncontrollable sobbing when the city came into view. "O Jerusalem, Jerusalem, thou that killest the prophets, and stonest them which are sent unto thee, how often would I have gathered thy children together, even as a hen gathereth her chickens under her wings, and ye would not" (Matt. 23:37). Then with a mourner's wail, Jesus pronounced doom upon the city, upon the nation, and upon her religion.

Shall we not, like our Savior, reach out to our blind, senseless world? As we hear the death rattle in the throat of our civilization, may we not mourn as at the death of a dear loved one? In spite of the rigor mortis of the church's spiritual life, shall we not try, with the balm of Gilead, to heal her heart? Shall we not pity her and help her? And, if in the just judgment of God, a twentieth-century institutionalized church goes down to rise no more, shall we not be the last to abandon the ship? And, like Jesus, never give up until the last ray of hope winks out.

7

THE MONEY CRISIS

Money! What is this thing called money? A piece of paper? Legal tender? A medium of exchange? That and more. Money is a symbol of wealth, of power and prestige. It is stored-up personality, the product of our labors and intelligence. It is an emblem of service and the result of a spent life.

What did Jesus have to say about this thing called money? Was he friend or foe? Did he condemn it or approve it?

Jesus did not condemn money as such. Money is a thing. His fight was with our greedy, coveteous spirit. Jesus did not approve carelessness as being Christian. He never condoned neglect. There is enough economic thought in the teachings of Jesus, if misapplied, to blow our society into smithereens.

Poverty is no assurance of godliness, and wealth is no guarantee of wickedness. Poverty may very well grind a man's soul into the dust, and rob him of his faith in God. A certain amount of goods is necessary to keep us free from want and depression and to allow some time for the enjoyment of life.

A prison commissioner said that "poverty and destitution are the root of most offenses against the law." The pinch of poverty embitters destitute men against an affluent society in whose wealth they do not share. They seek "their part" by robbing and looting.

Jesus knew that money could be useful. He told his disciples to "make friends for yourselves with worldly wealth" (Luke 16:9, TEV).[1] The Savior recognized that, although men could not serve God and mammon, they could serve God *with* mammon.

With money a man can aid the kingdom of God or degrade himself and his society. He can feed the hungry, clothe the naked, and heal the sick. He can build churches, hospitals, schools, and orphanages. Money can put the Bible in the hands of the world and preach the gospel to the poor.

Money can create beautiful things, or it can make a man's world into a living hell. The Samaritan's money paid the bill for a wounded stranger. Joseph of Arimathea's wealth gave Jesus a decent burial. Mary Magdalene's life savings anointed the Lord for his death. But the rich man's money blinded him to the beggar who lay at his gate. It destroyed Lazarus and sent Dives to hell.

Wealth, therefore, is both good and bad. If we use it as the servant of God and man, it is good. If it enslaves either us or our brother and separates us from God, it is bad. Money is:

> Dug from the mountain side
> or washed in the glen,
> Servant am I or master of men.
> Earn me, I bless you;
> Steal me, I curse you;
> Grasp and hold me
> A fiend shall possess you.
> Lie for me, die for me,
> Covet me, take me—
> Angel or devil,
> I'm just what you make me![2]

Jesus challenges our motives and devotion. Do we really want money for the sake of making a better life? Or does our greed for gold, and the power that comes with wealth drives us like galley slaves?

"I have to live, you know," can easily become a feeble covering for a multitude of greedy sins.

Seeking security can become an insatiable desire. The narcotic of money grips the soul, and a man is never satisfied however much he may possess. The drug of wealth dulls his higher sensibilities, and money-making takes precedence over all else. He is as dissatisfied with ten thousand dollars as he was with one. If he reaches a hundred thousand or perchance a million, he is even less satisfied and less secure. For a craving gets hold upon his heart, and he covets nothing but wealth. He becomes the victim of a strange poverty that plagues him with fears of want in the midst of plenty.

My mother used to say, "Men will not go to hell for a dollar but they will fool around the brink after a nickel until they fall in."

Jesus knew well that wealth could easily become a man's God. Therefore, he warned the disciples that they could not serve two masters. God and mammon travel in opposite directions. We cannot follow them both. The direction we take is a moral one, and each of us decides which it shall be. For the love of money gnaws at the soul of all men. Station in life gives no immunity from the specter of greed. None ever arrives at the point where he has enough.

Wealthy Andrew Carnegie said, "Some men think that poverty is a dreadful burden, and that wealth leads to happiness. What do they know about it? They know only one side; they imagine the other. I have lived both, and I know there is little in wealth that can add to human happiness beyond the small comforts of life."

Nero exhausted every conceivable pleasure, and offered prizes for suggestions of new entertainments. He ruled the world's mightiest empire. His porches were a mile long, and the ceiling of his banquet hall sprinkled his guests with perfume and rose petals. He wore a crown worth half a million, and his mules were shod with silver. Yet Nero was gloomy, peevish, miserable, dissatisfied, and died a suicide.

Alexander the Great was born to one empire and conquered another. He possessed the wealth of both the East and the West. Yet he commanded that when carried to his grave his hands should be left unwrapped and outside the bier so that all men might see them empty.

The deceitfulness of riches blinds us to life's true values. We trade eternal things for things that are temporary and swap the soul for the body. We become niggardly with our means, and generosity cankers within us. The evil shadow of greed drapes its dark mantle between us and our God. What might have been a mansion in heaven turns out to be a mud hut in hell. Our lives that could have been opened up to the fullness of God here and his glories hereafter become pinched and shriveled. We, like the rich Englishman, shuffle about the streets in our old age muttering, "Money, money, money."

Jesus' concern was that we laid too much stress on temporary and trivial things. We come to believe that our life *does* consist in the abundance of things we possess. We develop a "money brain" which, in our western culture, is the supreme brain. We get to believing we *can* live by bread alone. Our world inverts itself. Side issues take center stage. Raiment and meat take precedence over body and soul. Riches become pride, pride becomes independence, and independence becomes practical atheism. We are robbed of our desire and ability to worship God. Appetite destroys soul, and making a living consumes life.

Jesus' point was, "What *place* shall we give things?" What shall we call "essential" and what shall be secondary? The fever with which we pursue spiritual or material goals becomes the accurate thermometer of our lives. Where our treasure is, there will our hearts be also.

In our heated pursuit of wealth, we do not stop to consider

what we are sacrificing to get it. We become needlessly preoccupied with material things. Communion with God grows difficult. We turn a deaf ear to the cries of men. And, like Martha, we are anxious and troubled about many things.

"Fool," said Jesus of the wealthy farmer. (We would have called him prudent, a good manager.) He was rich in this world's goods and poverty-stricken in spirit. He preferred body to soul, the world to God, and time to eternity. He built a great business here and lived a pauper hereafter.

When the English man-of-war, *Britannia*, wrecked off the coast of Brazil, she was carrying a hundred kegs of silver. At the time of the wreck several kegs were brought on deck to try to save them. Seeing the ship breaking up so quickly, the sailors climbed into the lifeboats, leaving the fortune behind. One sailor returned to the ship to see if all were safely off. There on the deck he found a shipmate who had broken open several kegs and was sitting in a pile of silver.

"What are you doing?" shouted the midshipman. "Don't you know this vessel is breaking up and will go down any minute?"

"Let her go," replied the fool. "I've lived a poor wretch all my life, and I'm determined to die rich."

Ruskin's judgment of the English is too often a judgment of the whole race: "The first of all English games," he said, "is *making money*. . . . We knock each other down oftener in playing at that than at football, or any other rougher sport." A little silver changes window to a mirror, and we see only ourselves rather than our brothers.

Jesus knew that wealth made true brotherhood difficult if not impossible. So when the rich young ruler asked to join his band of disciples, Jesus asked him to come down to their level. "Get rid of your wealth, and then come," said Jesus. He would not. His actions more than justified Jesus' estimate of the man. As someone has said, "When a man gets wealth, God either gets a servant, or the man loses his soul."

The money motive has caused men to grind their brothers into the dust and exact a fortune at the price of human slavery. Children of only six years old have been worked in sweat shops from 9 A.M. to 9 P. M. Naked young girls have been used to haul coal underground like animals. Homes have been jerked out from under the poor by heartless financiers. Black men have been bought and sold like cattle.

Judas—greedy, selfish Judas—stole the common fund that bought food for the disciples, and he sold his Master for the price of a slave. Black deed? Certainly. But how many Judases are still with us today? They cheat their brothers and betray their Lord. And for what? Money.

If a man can make a million and keep his sense of brotherhood with man and partnership with God, well and good. But if, in the process of making money, he loses sight of who owns title to his property and shuts his heart up to his brother, he has lost all that life was made for.

Jesus did not live in isolation from the temptations of wealth. He was a man, and he lived with all the temptations of men. He could have turned stones to bread, or for that matter, to gold, diamonds, emeralds; but something held more importance for Jesus than the belly. And he would not sell his soul for a loaf of bread.

The Savior had the unique ability to make one thing the center of his life. That one thing was the kingdom of God. He subordinated every other desire to that supreme loyalty, but we are different. Our lives are a hodgepodge of conflicting loyalties. They are like the careless student's textbook. Everything is emphasized and underlined and nothing ends up being emphasized. We try to give top priority to both God and money, and neither gets top priority.

We soon discover that Jesus was exactly right. We cannot serve two masters. To the extent that we choose the one, we must

forswear allegiance to the other. The pursuit of wealth and the
pursuit of spiritual life are not compatible. A man could as well
spend eternity with one foot in heaven and the other in hell as to
serve God and mammon.

Life is like the solar system. God must be at the center with
other things finding their place around him. Otherwise, everything is out of kilter. Desires wander to and fro, banging into
each other, creating chaos in our lives. It was for this reason that
Jesus said, "Seek ye first the kingdom of God, and his righteousness; and all these things shall be added unto you" (Matt. 6:33).

A little girl kept bothering her dad as he tried to read the morning paper. Finally, he hit upon a plan to keep her busy. There in
the paper was a map. He cut it into several pieces, mixed them up,
and handed them to his daughter. "Here, put the world back together," he said. She went away, and in a few minutes she was
back with the map in perfect order.

He was amazed. "How on earth did you do that?" he cried.
"Well, daddy," she replied, "you see there was a picture of Jesus
on the other side. I knew when I got Jesus in the right place,
the world would be in the right place."

Jesus challenged all that was current coin in the economic theology of his day. Wealth was not proof of God's approval, and
poverty was not a sign of his judgment. Rather, the poor were
blessed; but the rich found it impossible to get into the kingdom
of God. An outcast Samaritan helped with his money while a
wealthy priest passed by on the other side. A rich man went to
hell, and a beggar was carried by the angels to Abraham's bosom.
The poor widow who cast only two mites into the Temple treasury
cast in more than the wealthy.

Men were to share their possessions with those in need. Their
treasures were to be laid up in heaven, not upon the earth. And
wealth must not be allowed to usurp the place of God. "For that
which is highly esteemed among men is abomination in the sight

of God. (Luke 16:16).

Jesus' philosophy was, "Whosoever of you will be the chief-est, shall be servant of all" (Mark 10:44). But we reject his teach-ing and live by the motto, "Whosoever will be chiefest, let him be richest of all." We push off onto others Jesus' teachings about the ravens that neither sow nor reap and the lilies that spin not. Such stuff may be very well for religious folk, but we do not generally accept it for ourselves. And this trust in a God who knows our needs may do very well when the opportunity for getting is gone. But for the present, it is only religion.

Not laboring for "the food that perishes, but for the food which endures to eternal life" is fine for preachers, priests, and mission-aries. But it is altogether out of place in the modern business world. Laying up treasures in heaven may be well and good for the aged and infirm. It may be of some consolation for those too poor to have treasures upon earth. But for the average churchman, it is "ivory tower" philosophy. "Too impractical for real life," we say.

We give Sunday morning lip service to the Beatitudes. Ah, we do like them well for sermonizing in our multimillion-dollar sanc-tuaries. But our hearts are far from them. In real life we reject them as sentiment or overstatement of the case. Our theology goes more like this: "Blessed are the wealthy, the well-fed, and the aggressive." We are especially strong on the wealthy if we *are* one of them. We may agree that the poor are blessed if we *are not* one of them, but to recite responsively in a church ritual the Beati-tudes does seem to make a conscience burdened with silver a bit lighter, doesn't it?

When we have fully searched out the sayings of Jesus on money and have made all our excuses, the Lord's warnings still hang over the head of wealth like the sword of Damocles. Jesus warned men more often against covetousness than against the vices of adultery, fornication, lying, and theft. (I wonder why our pulpits are so silent on this sin?)

Anglican Bishop Gore said, "There is more in the Gospels against being rich and in favor of being poor than most of us like to recognize." But the words of Jesus fall harsh on the ears of an affluent western society. We prefer to charge him with using Oriental hyperbole. Or we suggest that his words were "ideal" and must be modified for modern culture. They pinch our consciences at the point of our pocketbooks, and we call them too radical. But our theological backflips do not get us off the hook.

Theologians tell us that Jesus' words were for a "definite situation" and have no "permanent validity." They are "unique" and are not to become generalized rules for Christian living. Luke is biased in favor of the poor. Jesus is deluded by the immediate approach of the end. Therefore he speaks from an "apocalyptic orientation."

Bosh! Why don't we just admit our sins of greed, and admit that Jesus was absolutely right. Coveteousness subverts more souls than any other sin. The unequal distribution of wealth is the primary cause for social evils and international strife.

Walter Rauschenbush, Baptist theologian, said, "It gives a touch of cheerful enjoyment . . . to watch the athletic exercises of interpreters when they confront these sayings of Jesus about wealth. They find it almost as hard to get around the needle's eye as the camel would find to get through."

I have no doubt that if Jesus were here today he would revise much of our financial theology. And we, like the disciples, would be exceedingly amazed."

For no greater sin exists in the Christian church today than its use or misuse of its wealth. Millions are being poured into magnificent structures, pipe organs, carpets, and chandeliers—elaborate testimonials to our affluence and spiritual stagnation. Salaries of professional religious managers run into five figures, a situation that is hardly compatible with the Galilean and his fisherman disciples. Within the shadows of our cathedrals and towering spires, multitudes live in subsistence poverty and go without the gospel witness. I have an uncomfortable feeling that were the Lord here, he would once again drive the money changers from the Temple. Nothing provoked the wrath of Jesus like profiteering in the house of God.

The Savior is not pleased when the church floats a million dollar bond issue for a building and fails to feed a hungry man a bowl of soup or give a cold child a warm coat. Small wonder we are spiritually impoverished. The church has lost her soul in search of things.

On one of his pilgrimages to Rome, Thomas Aquinas saw the vast wealth of the Vatican. As they walked past the chests of gold, the pope said to him, "No longer do we have to say, 'Silver and gold have we none.' " "Neither," replied the saint, "can we say, 'In the name of Jesus, rise up and walk.' "

No greater need exists than for the church to rediscover Jesus' thoughts and teachings on money and then to apply his teachings to the real life situation. For we have not yet, even in the church, escaped the legacy of selfishness. Indeed, the times Christianity has been used to justify slavery and human exploitation have not been few. "The Bible says," we have cried; taking a Scripture text to justify our sins. But our real motive has been simply *money*.

Jesus' challenge to our age is not so much to conquer outer space as it is to come to terms with the inner man. Our faith must affect our desire for and our use of money. Life does not have to be an endless alteration between strain for wealth and search for diversion. We have astonished the world with the things we've done. But we have no inner resources, and when we are alone the poverty of our souls stares us in the face. We have lost our way, and wandered away from God in the maze of material things. Now we are at the mercy of our idolatrous cravings.

Wordsworth described us well when he said:

"The world is too much with us; Late and soon,
        Getting and spending, we lay waste our powers:
        Little we see in Nature that is ours;
    We have given our hearts away, a sordid boon!"

We have proved Jesus absolutely right. We have profited nothing. We have gained the world and lost our soul. We are filled with a hateful human pride that takes all God gives; forgets the Giver; clutches wealth to its breast; and cries, "Mine." We have turned our eyes in upon ourselves and said, "My power and the might of mine hand hath gotten me this wealth" (Deut. 8:17). What fools we are to set our hearts on things we cannot ultimately keep and go off to our graves, a poor misshapen thing, ill prepared for eternity.

——————

1. From *Today's English Version* of the New Testament. Copyright © American Bible Society, 1966, 1971.
2. Walter B Knight, *Knight's Master Book of New Illustrations* (Grand Rapids: Wm. Eerdmans Publishing Company, 1961), p. 575.

8

SHADOW OF THE CROSS

Silence settled over Calvary. The "hill of the skull" lay littered with human carnage. Vultures drifted overhead; sniffing the stench of dried blood and filling the air with their gluttonous screeches. The sun burned like a bronze disk in the Syrian sky. Ugly crevices left by the earthquake gaped here and there in the bleaching rocks. The wind kicked up wisps of dust, and the rocky face of the hill shimmered in the heat.

A few soldiers sat around, idly waiting for their victim to die. Only a half dozen or so bystanders still stayed to watch. Three gaunt crosses, bearing their burden of tortured human flesh, cast their eerie bony shadows toward the horizon.

One of the soldiers casually picked up a spear and shoved it into the side of the man on the middle cross. Blood and water poured out. Jesus was dead.

He died on a cross on a hill outside the walls of Jerusalem. Every Sunday School child knows that; but the question thoughtful men have been asking themselves since that dark Friday in A. D. 30 is, "Why?" Why did Jesus die at that time, in that way, and at that place?

He did not have to die. He could have fled and lived among the Gentiles. The Jews had already suggested that. He also had the power to give his life or to keep it. This right he had received from his Father. He could have commanded more than twelve legions of angels. Instantly heaven's host would have been at his side. He could have denied his claims as the Messiah and saved his life. He could even have cast his lot with the religious authorities or pleaded for clemency before Pilate, but the Savior did none of these. Rather he saw his death coming and made no effort to avoid it. He went voluntarily to his arrest, trial, and crucifixion.

Jesus did not have to die at Jerusalem. Other attempts had been made on his life, but all had failed. At Nazareth an enraged mob tried to throw him over a cliff. The scribes and Pharisees had often tried to stone him. You will recall Jesus' biting words as he journeyed to the last Passover, "It cannot be that a prophet perish out of Jerusalem" (Luke 13:33).

You see, he chose not only to die, but his place to die as well.

The Lord did not have to die on the cross. He did not come there by accident but by divine purpose and personal choice. The Savior often spoke of the way he would die. He must be "lifted up."

Jesus was not the victim of a sad set of circumstances. His death was not the final outcome of his clash with the Jews or his refusal to bow to Rome. It did not just happen that events conspired to bring him to a cross on Calvary. Nor did he go there out of some selfish, sick motive. Jesus died when he died, where he died, and how he died because he chose it that way.

Astronomers know long before the eclipse of the sun or moon that the shadows are racing across the heavens. So, Christ also saw the approaching shadow of the cross long before that fateful Passover. Jesus, more than any man in history, was born to die— to die at a particular place and in a particular way. From the dim and ancient past before the world was formed until the day he climbed up Calvary, the Savior knew what lay ahead.

From the day of his baptism, Jesus "steadfastly set his face to

go to Jerusalem" (Luke 9:51). At the Jordan he began his steady
march to Calvary. Though no man saw it, the shadow of the cross
hung across his path all the way. The weight of the timber never
left his shoulders until Simon lifted it in the way.

I am astonished that anyone could doubt that Jesus knew all
along he was going to die. Surely, no one could think he was
ignorant of the implications of John's introduction: "Behold, the
Lamb of God, which taketh away the sin of the world" (John 1:
29). Because from that hour onward he talked about his death
with his disciples, his friends, and his enemies.

His first public act, the cleansing of the Temple, was a prophecy
of things to come. There he ran head-on into entrenched, organized religion. There he revealed the ultimate outcome of that
clash. "Destroy this temple," he said, "and in three days I will
raise it up" (John 2:19).

His disciples did not understand then. And the Jews never
understood. But, after Calvary, his disciples recalled these words,
and realized he had made a cryptic prophecy of his death and
resurrection.

Remember his statement to Nicodemus? (This was during his
early Judean ministry.) "And as Moses lifted up the serpent in
the wilderness, even so must the Son of man be lifted up" (John
3:14). Don't you think Jesus knew what "lifted up" meant? Of
course. It was a common soft reference to crucifixion, much like
we say "deceased' for "died."

Later on he said to the multitudes, "And, I, if I be lifted up
from the earth, will draw all men unto me" (John 12:32). They
understood. For they said in astonishment, "We have heard out
of the law that Christ abideth for ever: and how sayest thou,
The Son of man must be lifted up?" (John 12:34). Then John
added a note that Jesus said this to indicate the kind of death he
was to die.

But, remember what Moses and Elijah were talking about on the mount of transfiguration? The Savior's departure, his death, which he was about to accomplish at Jerusalem. Now, to say that Moses and Elijah knew what lay ahead and Jesus did not is so foolish that it beggars the imagination.

Too, read Jesus' prayer in John 17. Notice the very first words out of his mouth: "Father, the hour is come; glorify thy Son, that thy Son also may glorify thee" (v. 1). The rest of that prayer concerns two things—his death and his disciples.

As the Savior neared the close of his ministry, the storm clouds of hate and prejudice rolled in. The plot to kill him took final shape. Jesus knew that at the coming Passover the dam would burst. The pent-up anger and bitterness of the Pharisees would roll in over his soul like an angry flood and sweep him up to Calvary. His hour had come. His appointment with the cross must be kept. And the disciples must be prepared. But such an impossible job it was.

Over and over again, Jesus warned them that "the Son of man shall be delivered into the hands of men" (Luke 9:44). Over and again it is written, "But they understood not this saying" (Luke 9:45).

Poor men! Of course they did not understand. They could not get hold of the idea that the Messiah of Israel would die, especially by Roman crucifixion. They were shocked or should I say appalled by such talk. Listen to Jesus flatly tell them that "he must go unto Jerusalem, and suffer many things of the elders and chief priests and scribes, and be killed, and be raised again the third day" (Matt. 16:21).

All the disciples but Peter sat in stunned silence. And he spoke when he should have kept silent. "Killed! The Messiah, the King of Israel, be killed?" Impossible! It was too much. He had to be mistaken. They would not allow it. It was not until the event actually took place that they could accept it as reality.

I suppose, though the disciples immediately dismissed this whole business of dying. For a few days later they got into a fuss over political appointments in the coming kingdom. James and John put in their bid for the choicest positions—one on the right hand and the other on the left. Had they only known what being on his right hand and on his left meant, they would not have been so hasty. On his right hand and on his left stood two crosses bearing two cursing, dying thieves.

Jesus would not let these men by with their blindness. Six days later he was transfigured before their very eyes. "This is it," thought his disciples. Peter jumped in and said, "Let us make here three tabernacles; one for thee, and one for Moses, and one for Elias (Matt. 17:4). (If Jesus had wanted to establish a material kingdom, Peter would have made a grand chief of staff.) There were to be no tabernacles and no earthly kingdoms. The Savior must go down from the mount.

What's more, he starting talking again about going to Jerusalem, suffering many things from the elders and chief priests, and being killed. But did his words sink in this time? Not at all. As they went down to the valley, they were wondering what all this loose talk about dying meant.

Jesus began his last journey to Jerusalem. His appointment with death awaited him there, and he wanted to be on time. A strange air surrounded him. A solemn look fell across his face. He quickened his pace, walking ahead of his men. They noticed it and were afraid.

From here on, Jesus spoke more openly to his disciples. He challenged the authority of perverted, entrenched religion more fervently. The tempo of the conflict increased; tensions mounted; the hatred of the Jews burned white hot. Jesus knew it would only be a matter of time before civilized restraint would give way under the strain of frustration, anger, and the thirst for revenge. The smell of death hung in the air. Jerusalem was in a ferment. The Jews had reached their decision—Jesus must die. The machinery to bring him to the cross had been set in motion.

Keep in mind, however, that Jesus was not an unwilling victim, walking ignorantly into their trap. Judas' betrayal, the lies of the false witnesses, and a quisling Pilate were not news to him. His hour had come. He knew it, and he stepped calmly toward the "hill of the skull."

At last, during the final few hours of his life, the idea that he was going to die hit home to his disciples. Even then, they hoped for a turn in events. Peter prepared to fight it out in the garden. Really, it was not until they were seated around the table at the last Passover that the light, or should I say night, dawned on these twelve men.

Don't forget, Jesus had warned them from the first that the bridegroom must be taken away. He had pointed out to them that he would die at Jerusalem on a cross. He would be betrayed into the hands of sinners. They would condemn him to death and deliver him to the Gentiles for scourging and execution. He had even reminded them that Mary's precious ointment was the anointing oil for his burial.

At the visit of the Greeks, Jesus declared, "The hour is come, that the Son of man should be glorified" (John 12:23). He told his disciples that he was going away, and where he was going they could not come.

Yet it was not until Jesus said, "I came forth from the Father, and am come into the world: again, I leave the world, and go to the Father" (John 16:28), that they finally understood. They suddenly said, "Lo, now speakest thou plainly" (John 16:29). I'm sure Jesus thought, I've spoken plainly for a long time. You just haven't listened.

Jesus *had* spoken to them in figurative speech. Many of the forecasts of his death were of this nature, but he tells them why: "These things I said not unto you at the beginning, because I was with you. But now I go my way to him that sent me"

(John 16:4). The disciples did not need to know too much too soon. But his hour had arrived, and they must have it straight.

Jesus even told the multitudes of his coming death. Remember how he said to them, "Whoso eateth my flesh, and drinketh my blood, hath eternal life" (John 6:54)? He said also to them, "I am the good shepherd: the good shepherd giveth his life for the sheep" (John 10:11).

I doubt that they knew what he meant. But no one today could doubt that he spoke of his death.

Jesus often told his enemies that he knew what they were about to do. He told them that he was going away, and that they would seek him and would not find him. Where he was going they could not come. In their ignorance they thought he was going to be a Messiah to the Gentiles or else kill himself.

Remember the heated debate between Jesus and the Jews in the Temple treasury? Jesus said to them, "When ye have lifted up the Son of man, then shall ye know that I am he" (John 8:28). He even bluntly told them, "Ye seek to kill me" (v. 37).

You see, Jesus' death came as no surprise to him. He had known about it from the beginning. Those who heard him would have known it too if they had listened, but their minds were closed. They would not hear.

What Jesus suffered was not put upon him. He took it up of his own free will. Over and over again, he said, "Mine hour is not yet come" (John 12:23). What a splendid illustration of his control over his destiny!

I resent the rude insinuation that Jesus was a helpless pawn of circumstances. The might of Rome did not snatch away his life. The conniving of the Jews did not finally corner him at the Passover in Jerusalem. Pilate and Caiaphas had no power at all over him but what had been given them from heaven. Had Jesus not been willing to go to the cross, nothing on earth and no power from hell could have sent him there.

During the last few days of his life, Jesus' enemies encircled him. They closed in, and Judas snapped the trap shut. But Jesus was not accidentally caught in the jaws of a well-laid plan. He harbored no uncertainty about what lay ahead.

He finished his prayer in Gethsemane and quietly said to his disciples, "Rise up, let us go" (Mark 14:42). He asked that his disciples be let go so that they would not have to suffer with him. He then challenged his captors: "Why do you come with your clubs and staves? Do you think I will resist arrest? Haven't I been among you all along? Shall I run out now?"

His surrender was so bold that his enemies were knocked backward. See, he was in complete control. Lies and trickery brought him to his death, but not without his consent. Jesus faced the ultimate outcome of his life in serene and undivided loyalty to God. Listen to him as he prayed, "Now is my soul troubled; and what shall I say? Father, save me from this hour: but for this cause came I unto this hour" (John 12:27). "Put up thy sword into the sheath," Jesus told Peter. "The cup which my Father hath given me, shall I not drink it?" (John 18:11).

Our Savior refused the wine and the gall on the cross. He needed no mind-dulling narcotic to brace him for the last battle. Jesus was dying for sinners. He wanted to do it with an alert mind. He was going home. He wanted to go with his soul awake and eyes wide open.

When the hour came for Sir Walter Raleigh's execution, he laid aside his gown, and called to the headsman to show him the ax. The headsman was a bit slow, and the philosopher called out, "I prithee let me see it. Dost thou think that I am afraid of it?" He passed his thumb over the razor edge and said to the sheriff, "This is a sharp medicine, but a sound cure for all diseases." Kissing the blade, he laid it down.

After this, he went to the corners of the scaffold, knelt down, and prayed with his people. He then began to fit himself for the block. First, he laid himself down to see how the block fit. The executioner rushed up and begged his forgiveness. Raleigh embraced him and gave orders for him not to strike until he gave the sign. Then he laid his head down to receive the fatal stroke. His executioner asked that he face the east. "It matters not," replied Raleigh, "which way a man's head faces as long as his heart is right with God."

Placing his beard out of the way, Raleigh raised his hand to signal the headsman. Either in fear or absentmindedness, the man hesitated. Raleigh put up both hands and cried, "Why dost thou not strike? Strike, man, strike!"

The blade flashed in the sun, and in two blows the martyr was in eternity. His body never shrank from the spot. But, like his noble mind, remained immovable.

Now, do you think that Jesus, upon whom Raleigh and the whole world pinned their hopes, died in any less noble fashion?

Jesus knew from the beginning that his death was absolutely essential to the fulfillment of his mission. He had come to save men from sin. And he knew before he stepped foot upon this earth that without the shedding of blood there is no remission. He died in the complete assurance that because he died, others would not have to die. He chose the cross, deliberately and unselfishly; he chose it and all its horrors. He fully expected to accomplish something by his death that would have been impossible without it.

E. Y. Mullins, once president of Southern Baptist Seminary, said, "Something befell Christ, and by reason of that, the something need not befall sinners."

A frightful price for our sins, you say. Certainly! But a lesser price would not do. The famous Anglican churchman, R. C. Trench wrote, "When God chose the costliest means of our deliverance, . . . we may be quite sure that at no lower price could our redemption have been possible."

Christ was not content to sit comfortably on his throne while we wallowed in our sins. He saw us, lost and straying. Our lostness drew him like a magnet from heaven to earth, from his glory to his shame, from his crown to his cross.

And men may debate about whether Jesus was right or wrong about the purpose for which he died. But none can argue about the purpose for which Jesus *believed* he was dying. He was dying to complete what he had started—seeking and saving that which was lost.

Jesus wept over stiffnecked, stubborn Jerusalem. She shut her eyes to the day of her salvation and walked blindly into the jaws of God's judgment. She turned from the light and stumbled over the precipice of destruction. Was she more blind than we? Was her heart any harder than ours? We have had over nineteen hundred years of the gospel and still we stumble and fall into the bottomless pit, doubting and disputing about why Jesus died.

There is a picture of the crucifixion painted by a celebrated artist. It is an after scene. The body of the Savior has been removed for burial. The cross lies on the ground. A band of little children are bending over the signs of the earth's bloodiest deed. One child holds in his hand a nail that a few hours before had held the hand or the foot of Christ to the cross. The child stands spellbound with horror, gazing at the bloody spike. Upon the face of all the children is the look of awe and terror that innocence must always cast upon that dreadful scene.

How did Jesus feel about this fearful moment? Did he cringe from it? He must have for he was human as well as divine. His soul recoiled as the traitorous lips of Judas brushed his cheek. His sense of justice revolted as the ugly mob surrounded him in Gethsemane. His mind shrank back at the sight of his bloody back, torn by the scourge, and his brow punctured by a wreath of twisted thorns. His face ached from the pounding the soldiers had given him with their fists. Spit dripped down his beard, turning him sick at his stomach. The muscles of his arms and legs jerked as the spikes tore through flesh and bone. Pain shot through his body as his limbs grew rigid and circulation was cut off. His ears rang with the bloodthirsty shout, "Crucify, crucify, crucify." Loneliness swept over his soul as the sun grew dark and the earth quaked. His plea, "My God, my God, why hast thou forsaken me?" joined nature's protest as the heavens bellowed out their agony with thunder and lightning.

Even Jesus could not tolerate that monstrous scene without being horrified by it. Peter's curses, the blood-soaked robe, the crude jokes of the crowd—all of it swam before his eyes.

He felt hell's hot breath blowing in his face. He heard the snide remarks of the soldiers, "Hail, King of the Jews!" and the mockings of the passersby, "Thou that destroyest the temple, and buildest it in three days, save thyself. If thou be the Son of God, come down from the cross" (Matt. 27:40). The pious religious leaders added their sick wit, "He saved others; himself he cannot save. If he be the King of Israel, let him now come down from the cross, and we will believe him. He trusted in God; let him deliver him now, if he will have him" (vv. 42-43).

Jesus knew, though, that his death was but a line at which the little streams of his life would flow into the great ocean of eternity. Like the Dutch martyr whose body was being licked by the flames, Jesus knew that his death was "a small pain compared to the glory to come."

His death was not the hour of his defeat. It was the hour of his triumph. What kind of victor was this? His crown was a hand full of thorns, his scepter a reed, his throne a scourging post, his procession mocking soldiers and jeering crowds. His arch of triumph was the way of sorrows; his coronation, crucifixion; his royal robes, a bloody tunic. His only benefactors were a lone disciple, a few weeping women, and a stranger who carried his cross.

This victor was alone in a sea of hostile faces as he dragged his cross, bumping and scraping, over the stone-paved streets. The only hands that ministered to his body were the bloody fingers of a Roman soldier that held the spikes while he drove them in place. His only acclamation was a note written in jest: "The King of the Jews."

As Jesus died, the mist rose from his Father's face. Darkness fled. The struggle was over; his work was finished. He emerged from the condemnation of sin and the terrors of hell. Christ's sensitive constitution gave way. He lifted his face to heaven with a whisper of victory—"It is finished." Then he, with his last breath, commended his spirit to his Father.

Jesus was dead. No, not dead. Christ, the man was dead. But the God-Christ was alive forevermore and has the keys of hell and of death.

Jesus is, in the face of all things apparently to the contrary, the victor. As Taylor said, "Not only does the cross tower o'er the wrecks of time, it towers over everything else that interests man."

His death signaled the final triumph of good over evil. It was the last stroke of God's pen in the story of man's salvation.

Why should the Savior stay on in this world? To go back to the Father was his deepest desire. As God's hand lifted the darkness, he slipped away home.

Emperor Theodosius once opened all the prisons and released the prisoners. Then he cried, "Oh, would to God that I now could open the graves and let the dead go free."

Jesus Christ can do just that. For as Luther said, "*Vivit! Vivit!* (He lives! He lives!)." And he lends us his victory shout, "O death, where is thy sting? O grave, where is thy victory?" (1 Cor. 15:55).

Jesus went not, as William Bryant says in "Thanatopsis":

> ". . . like the quarry-slave at night,
> Scourged to his dungeon, but sustained and soothed
> By an unfaltering trust, approach thy grave
> Like one who wraps the drapery of his couch
> About him, and lies down to pleasant dreams."

He went to the cross with the firm assurance that beyond death lay life; beyond his crucifixion lay his crown. He spoke of his death and resurrection in the same breath, and went to Calvary fully expecting to rise on the third day. For the sin, the ignorance, and the suffering of that dreadful day would not write the final chapter in the life of the Son of God.

Evening settled over the land. The shadow of the empty cross stretched across the hill and out toward the horizon. Jesus' two friends, Joseph of Arimathea and Nicodemus, gave him a decent burial.

But for Jesus,

> "'The tomb is not an endless night.
>   It is a thoroughfare—in a way
>   That closes in a soft twilight,
>   And opens in eternal day.'"

The curtain fell on Golgotha to rise on the empty tomb. The Man who suffered rose from the grave. Forty days later he ascended to his throne in the heavens. From there we look for him to return as the all-victorious King of kings and Lord of lords.

Until then, let us join Renan in his anthem of praise:

"Rest now in thy glory, noble initiator. Thy work is completed; thy divinity is established. Fear no more to see the edifice of thy effort crumble through a flaw. Henceforth, beyond the reach of frailty, thou shalt be present, from the height of thy divine peace, in the infinite consequences of thy acts. At the price of a few hours of suffering, which have not even touched thy great soul, thou hast purchased the most complete immortality. For thousands of years the world will extol thee. Banner of our contradictions, thou wilt be the sign around which will be fought the fiercest battles. A thousand times more living, a thousand times more loved since thy death than during the days of thy pilgrimage here below, thou wilt become to such a degree the corner-stone of humanity, that to tear thy name from this world would be to shake it to its foundations. Between thee and God, men will no longer distinguish. Complete conqueror of death, take possession of thy kingdom, whither by the royal road thou has traced, ages of adorers will follow thee.[1]

———

1. Ernest Renan, *The Life of Jesus* (A. L. Burt Company, Publishers, 1863, pp. 368-69.

9

THE RETURN

In 1904, A. H. Strong said, "Faith in a second coming of Christ has lost its hold upon many Christians in our day." But how different his day was from ours. A. Cleveland Cox expressed it:

> "We are living, we are dwelling
>> In a grand and awful time,
> In an age on ages telling;
>> To be living is sublime."

Men everywhere are asking, "What does it all mean? Will we soon destroy ourselves? Is the end of time near?"

The answer to their question is so simple a schoolchild can understand it. The King is coming, coming in power and love to reign. And the death struggles of this age are the birthpangs of the new age to come. These are but the dark hours that precede the dawn of his return.

Our age is like the age of Noah, completely secularized. It is the hour when men "think not." We are preoccupied with earthly existence, and eternity escapes us. But the first faint sounds of the trumpet are beginning to fall on our ears. And there has never been a better time to take fresh stock of Jesus' return.

The only real question left to be answered is, "When?" Will he come in our lifetime? Could be. Signs of his approach multiply. The pink flush of his return is beginning to light up the eastern sky.

Our world is concussed by the mind-shattering power of sin. The trauma of worldwide calamities and threatening catastrophe has drained the lifeblood from our senses. And we stagger under an immense burden of social and personal problems. Bethlehem bristles with troops, and Israel lies in the eye of a hurricane of Arab hostility. The race trembles at the monstrous weapons of war buried in the bosom of the earth. The judgments of "The Revelation" are now capable of literal fulfillment.

But do not be afraid. Jesus is coming. Remember how he said, "And if I go . . . , I will come again" (John 14:3)? Think, too, of these words, "When ye shall see all these things, know that it is near, even at the doors" (Matt. 24:33). So, lift up your heads and look up. Your redemption draweth nigh.

Jim Vaus flew his light plane into a blinding thunderstorm. The clouds were black and mean-looking. Rain was so heavy it would have floated a boat. The wings of the plane vibrated like guitar strings.

He said, "If you had been with me, you would have said, 'Jim, let's go back!' "

"But," said he, "these facts of the storm were not all the facts. Over the radio came the voice of the Miami center calling, '10JV—ID.' " He said, "I pushed the button of my radar transponder and in a few moments the Miami center came back and said, '10JV—radar contact. You'll be out of the storm cell in three minutes, and after that it is clear all the way.' "

This is the message of Christ to us. Now we are in the storm cell. The clouds are angry and mean. The words of Jesus come to us saying, "You'll be out of the storm cell in a little while, and after that it is clear all the way."

In times like these every man becomes a prophet. The universal cry goes up, "Lo, here, or lo, there." Church bulletins blaze with heralds of the end. But when the day of the Lord dawns, no announcement will be necessary. His coming will be as public as a bolt of lightning that splits the sky from east to west.

But our day is not much different from Jesus' day. The clouds of Roman vengeance hung low on the horizon. The thunder of her legions rumbled in the distance. The lightning of a hundred thousand swords flashed in the sun. Their target? Jerusalem.

Small wonder, then, the disciples were anxiously asking Jesus, "Tell us, when shall these things be? and what shall be the sign of thy coming, and of the end of the world?" (Matt. 24:3). They peered into the future, hoping for a ray of light, a word of hope. "Lord, wilt thou at this time restore again the kingdom to Israel?" they asked.

You and I share their hopes and fears. Their question is our question, "When, Lord?"

Jesus had a word for these frightened, uncertain men. "Take heed that no man deceive you" (Matt. 24:4). "It is not for you to know the times or the seasons, which the Father hath put in his own power" (Acts 1:7).

Jesus warned them to be careful about prying into tomorrow, curiously peeping into every calamity to see if they could see some sign of the end. Don't spend your time fumbling around with the future, but get on with your work and leave these things in your Father's care.

Does this mean Christ entertained any uncertainty about his return? Absolutely not. He left the Mount of Olives in the perfect assurance that he would come again. He did, however, quietly refrain from setting any dates, or arranging his itinerary. In fact, he plainly told his disciples that "of that day and hour knoweth no man, no, not the angels of heaven, but my Father only" (Matt. 24:36). Except for a passing mention or two, he said nothing about his return until the last week he lived on earth.

False Christs will arise. Wars, rumors of war, famine, earthquakes, unrest, and lawlessness will plague the world. Kingdom will rise against kingdom, nation against nation. But do not be troubled. All these things must come to pass, but the end is not yet. "All these things are the beginning of sorrows" (see Matt. 24:6-8).

Calamities in the social order and catastrophes in the natural order are the death throes of a world diseased and broken by sin. Do not fear them. Like contrails in the sky that mark the passing of a jet, these groanings of the last days are the lengthened shadow of the approach of the Son of man.

These events are like a ball whirling on a string. As the string gets shorter, the ball whirls faster and faster. Likewise, these evidences of the passing away of this present world order are beginning to show themselves with greater intensity and frequency.

Like the shadow of a man is cast before his coming, more frequent and violent wars, famines, earthquakes, pestilence, and upheavals in society are heralds of his coming.

It is altogether evident to anyone who cares to look that our aging world is showing more and more the ravages of sin. These "waymarks in the wilderness" are becoming more evident. And we will do well to keep watch.

Only a blind man or a fool could conclude that things are continuing as they were from the beginning of creation. But subtle and dramatic changes are taking place everywhere. If you listen carefully, you can hear his footfalls on the path.

No Christian can afford to sleep while the dull roar of the falls thunder in the distance. The movements of history, like the river's current, are picking up speed in preparation for the cataract of God's judgment.

You and I would do well to adopt Dr. Chapman's attitude toward Jesus' return. He said, "I never lay my head down at night except I think, "The Lord may come before daybreak." And I never rise in the morning except I think, 'The Lord may come before night falls.' " If we, like Dr. John A. Broadus, are "Always ready," then we shall be ready when he comes.

The approach of our Lord is like the building of a house. He did not want us to pack up at the first sound of the hammer. But he did tell us that when we saw the building taking final shape, the end was near.

Jesus wants us to live in constant expectancy of his return. He does not want us agitated into a keen sense of anticipation on Sunday only to be left hanging with a strange feeling of letdown when we find ourselves trudging back to the same old job on Monday. He wants us to be both pilgrims and permanent residents in the world, always prepared to stay but always keeping an eye on the eastern sky; "Looking for that blessed hope, and the glorious appearing of the great God and our Saviour Jesus Christ" (Titus 2:23).

There is no reason why we should go around clawing each other with disputes about our Lord's return. Too many are looking for labels to hang on one another, wasting their time in the witless art of building neat pigeonholes for each other's beliefs about the last days.

These senseless debates usually accomplish nothing and serve only to cloud the glory of the Lord's coming. It is a pity, that Jesus' return has become the most divisive issue among fundamental Christians.

Men have arranged charts covered with goblins, gargoyles, and wierd statues. They have expounded their slide-rule theology; taking the measurements of heaven, setting up an itinerary for the Savior's return, and establishing Christ as a glorified potentate surrounded by materialistic luxury and lashing out at his enemies until they are beaten into subjection.

There is no need to slash to ribbons Jesus' sayings about his return and then paste them back together to suggest our own private interpretations. Let Jesus speak plainly. Let him say what he wants to say. Then judge what all other men say by what he has said. Jesus has a better right than any other to know the details of his return.

You and I may have to give up some of our preconceived notions that have come from fiery preaching and modern prophets who are especially informed on the coming of the King. We may yet learn, if we carefully search the words of Jesus, to be honest with ourselves and true to the Scriptures. We may very well decide that a "suitable scheme of last things" is not nearly so important and may certainly be impossible to arrange. To be sure, let's not be guilty of prostituting the Word of God to some bizarre plan of our own. Keep in mind, too, that, had the Jews not been so sure *they* were correct, they would, no doubt, have recognized Jesus as their Messiah. An open mind and an upward look are the best preparation for the Savior's return.

God has left some things hidden from us. Leave them alone. They belong to him. Be satisfied to let him know some things you do not know.

Believe the things you can know and understand. Search for more light about the return of your Lord. When you find it, rejoice. Take the unknowns by faith. Trust them to your Father's care. He knows where he is going and when.

It is neither safe nor honest to go beyond what God has revealed, filling in the missing data and sketching in the missing parts of the pattern. For "the secret things belong unto the LORD our God: but those things which are revealed belong unto us and to our children for ever (Deut. 29:29).

Phillip Henry walked in on a tanner busily working at his bench. The tanner did not know Mr. Henry was there. When the tanner became aware of Mr. Henry's presence, he apologized for not knowing that he was in his shop.

Phillip Henry replied, "Then let Christ, when he comes, find me equally well employed in the duties of my calling."

It is not necessary to know the beginning and ending of the Lord's return to do that.

Simply take seriously Jesus' plain warnings about his return. Don't run after every crisis, thinking it is certainly *the* sign of the end. Stop sky-scanning and sign-seeking, making ill-founded forecasts of his coming. But, likewise, don't be lulled to sleep in the false notion that the Lord is delaying his return.

Rather, live like Sandy, a dim-witted lad in a country village in Scotland.

One dark December night, the heavens were filled with shooting stars. It seemed as if all creation were coming loose, and the end had come.

All the villagers, except Sandy, were awake, and scared out of their wits. Sandy's mother ran in, shook him, and cried, "Sandy, wake up. It is the Judgment Day."

Sandy leaped out of bed and cried, "Praise God, I'm ready."

Instead of indulging in gloomy forecasts about the future, we ought to share the expectancy of old Wisby.

His pastor called one day to make his usual visit to the old almshouse. Seated before the fireplace was an aged, withered couple. The old man was drawn over with disease, and palsy gripped his body. His shoes beat out a steady rhythm on the stone floor.

The pastor went up to the old man and shouted in his ear, "Well, Wisby, what are you doing?"

"Waiting, sir," replied Wisby.

"For what?" asked the pastor.

"For the appearing of my Lord, sir."

"And what makes you wait for the appearing of the Lord?"

"Because, sir, I expect great things then," said Wisby.

What excitement, what joy, what hope the return of our Savior ought to bring us. But, too often, our eyes are glued to the mire of the world. The church threatens to die, and all that good men try to do seems nullified by virulent evil.

We are like the mole who came up from his tunnel to hear the birds joyfully singing.

The mole asked, "What is there to sing about?"

The birds answered, "The sun is shining; flowers are blooming; the trees are green; and the grass is growing."

The mole, peering down into his burrow replied, "I don't see anything but darkness and worms."

Without a wholesome sense of Christ's return, our pessimism over things to come can increase until we will see little but chaos, failure, and darkness. Christ bids us look up. He calls us to lift our eyes above the horizon of this age and look toward eternity.

Kenneth Scott Latourette was right when he said, "It is clear that at the very beginning of Christianity there must have occurred a vast release of energy, unequalled in the history of the race." That burst of energy was generated, in part at least, by the disciples' keen expectancy of the immediate coming again of their Lord.

The chief center around which the early church rallied was the assurance that Jesus was coming again. It carried her through dungeon, fire, and sword. It made the damp catacombs glow with the warmth of Christ's presence. It turned defeat into victory, persecutions into cause for rejoicing, and caused an infant church of ignorant and unlearned men to cut like a broadsword across a pagan Roman Empire.

It drew the believers together in fellowship and dispersed them everywhere to preach the Word. They were certain that "the LORD saveth not with sword and spear: for the battle is the LORD's" (1 Sam. 17:47). They were constantly looking for the appearing of their Savior. Their last prayer was, "Even so, come; Lord Jesus."

In their hour of loneliness, distress, and disappointment, when the disciples had seen their Friend snatched from them, it was the message. "This same Jesus, which is taken up from you into heaven, shall so come in like manner as ye have seen him go into heaven" that raised their hopes and spirits. Jesus' own words, "I will go away, but you will see me again," came back to them in that dreadful hour.

The early church was like the young sailor who was making his first climb to the crow's nest. His shipmates watched as he neared the platform, high on the main mast. Suddenly, they froze with horror. The young seaman was looking down at the rolling ocean and swaying ship. He was getting dizzy and losing his grip.

In a chorus, they began to shout, "Look up. Matey, look up!"

When he heard their shout, the sick, dizzy sailor turned his eyes toward the calm, steady sky, and soon regained his balance.

What the shipmates cried to the young seaman, our returning Lord shouts to us, "Look up, Mates, look up!"

To the lament, "What is our world coming to?" the expectant Christian can say, "Not, 'What is our world coming to?' but, 'who is coming to our world?' " The final resolution of this age is not the doom of the world in a quagmire of inquity or in the fireball of a nuclear war. It is in the return of the King of kings and Lord of lords.

German evangelist George Mueller said, when the message of the return of Christ was first impressed upon his heart, "From my innermost soul I was stirred up to a feeling of compassion for sinners, and for the slumbering world around me, and I considered, 'Ought I not do what I can for the Lord Jesus while he tarries, and to arouse his slumbering Church.' "

No other dynamic can replace the faith that looks daily with an upturned face, filled with longing for the Lord's return. The urgency of human need, social challenge, the dynamic of evangelism—none of these can replace the power of an expectant waiting for the Savior's coming.

Without the assurance of the personal return of Christ, every